Good Earth Ga

A friendly guide to gr
organic vegetable~

Written and illustrated
by
Tim Foster

eco-logic books
practical solutions to environmental problems

First published in 2013
Revised, expanded, updated edition 2021

Copyright © text and illustrations: Tim Foster 2013, 2021

ISBN   978-1-899233-28-1

Cover illustration by Tim Foster
timfostergardener@gmail.com

Thanks to:

My grandfather, Albert Smith, for his special introduction to gardening. For instance, catching me in his greenhouse, he bellowed something like: "Get out of there, you little stinker, or I'll cut your ears off with the grape scissors." Grape scissors! Scissors just for grapes! A magical world opened up.

I'd also like to thank my parents and dedicate this to their memory, for allowing me to invade their garden and allotment when I was growing up, with activities that had only tenuous links to horticulture, like playing king of the castle on the compost heap.

I would like to thank all friends and family who have allowed me to practice the dark arts of gardening in their businesses and/or gardens over the years, and who still speak to me.

I must thank Mr. John Adler, publisher extraordinaire, who grew some vegetables with no help whatsoever and, though sadly no longer with us, is fondly remembered for getting this book underway and for an appalling sense of humour.

Many thanks to Peter Andrews of Ecologic Books for, despite trying to retire, still helping with this edition.

Thank you to Steve Palmer of i-sight design for his indispensable help and to Nigel Mitchell and Theresa Loosley of Biddles Books for its printing. All such valuable people.

And, of course, Melanie with my love.

Contents

Introduction

The main aim of this book is to provide an easily understandable guide to growing a range of common outdoor vegetables, organically.

Hopefully, there will be enough suitable information to inspire beginners to 'have a go'. For those of you who have already had a go, there is extra information to improve your techniques, or perhaps try something different. Along the way we can have an extremely jolly time.

It can be really fun trying to grow things. When polls are taken of occupations and happiness, horticulture hits the top spot most times. The need to be outside and connected with plants is in some way a part of our make-up. How could it not be after thousands of years of foraging and cultivating? Only in the past couple of hundred years have we moved away from this, and a lot of our modern-day malaises could be a connected to this link being broken.

Couple 'need' with 'fun' and 'health' and you have what could become a positively addictive pastime.

Lest you get carried away, be aware that there will be times when things don't turn out right. In some years, especially early on in your gardening career, it may be that more things fail than succeed. The secret here is to persevere: learn from the failure, celebrate the success, and record both. Next year you'll be even wiser, and hopefully more successful.

A wonderful feature of gardening is that no season is the same. The longer you grow things the easier you will find it to deal with anything that nature gently throws at you.

Maybe this book will be your guide to salvation. At some point in the not-too-distant future knowing how to grow your own food will become increasingly important, maybe even essential.

In any event, enjoy yourself.

Notes to the Second Edition

Well, I wasn't really expecting to go through this again but special requests, opportunities for extra / new information and, of course, a chance to correct a few errors (and make a few more) meant it was inevitable.

Few vegetables and chapters have remained unscathed – who says there is never anything new in gardening?

Hopefully, the basic approach remains, coupled with up-to-date information most of which is quite relevant.

Key to Information on Vegetables

Sowing Times

These vary according to the season and your location. If you are in a very favoured spot, you could be sowing a week or two ahead of the times shown. Similarly, the further north you go the later will be the sowing.

Sowing and Transplanting

Modules or cells refers to mini pots, all joined together - plastic compartments each with a drainage hole at the bottom – whose appearance is a little like an egg box, where each compartment or cell is used (usually) to raise a single plant. Such modules are readily available; the sturdier, and so reusable, the better. There's a section near the back on how to sow seeds either in modules, trays or nursery seedbeds – little areas of ground used just for raising plants before planting them out.

When it says 'direct' sowing, this simply means sowing the seeds in the ground where they will remain until harvest. The soil would have to be prepared: loosened, finely raked and made weed-free.

When it says 'place the seed on its edge': if you imagine the seed like a coin, it would be planted so that it could roll around.

Where it says: 'compost is used when planting', this means putting some in the planting hole and spreading around the plants once they are in. If compost is applied as a mulch, it is not dug in. It is applied to the surface where it is left.

Spacings

These should be the optimum for the highest yields and long-term health of the plants; the former relying on the latter to a certain degree.

Harvesting

When it says clear-cutting, this means cutting off everything that is there, to about 3cm above the ground, as in 'cutting' and 'clearing'.

Fertility

The rating 'High', 'Medium' or 'Low' gives an approximate requirement of the needs for each vegetable. For example: squash plants need a fairly high fertility to succeed, so the soil must be fed in anticipation of this. How you achieve this and what you use is an important feature of organic growing. Have a look at the 'Fertility' bit at the back of the book for more details.

Pests and Diseases

Every living thing is interacting with other living things, either positively or negatively; with vegetables, the negative ones are likely to be pests or diseases. For each vegetable, a short list of the worst P and D is provided. Refer to the P & D section towards the back for more detail. It is by no means comprehensive but will hopefully see you through most situations.

Varieties

Strictly speaking, we should be referring to 'cultivars', but let's not worry about that. Very few varieties are given here, mainly because what does well on my plot and what I think tastes terrific, may cause you to run a mile. Also new varieties are appearing each year. Your seed catalogue will tell you that everything is wonderful, so you'll just have to experiment a bit.

The few varieties I have selected have been around a while, are tried and tested and should still be available for years to come.

Comments

There may be a rare nugget of useful information hidden in here. These are the bits to read in an armchair with a cup of tea when it's too wet to be outside.

Stuff at the back

These are short chapters on some of the most important aspects of growing organically, with nifty techniques and other ramblings.

Beans, Broad

Vicia faba
(*Vicia*, Latin for vetch; *faba*, Latin for broad bean)
Family – PAPILIONACEAE

Sowing

When: Autumn – October to early November
Spring – March to April.
Where: Direct into a prepared bed.
How: Sow 5cm (2ins) deep, either in a zigzag 'band' 22.5cm x 22.5cm (9ins x 9ins), then 60cm (2ft) before another band; or evenly spaced at 30cm (12ins) in all directions.
Fertility: Low
Harvest: Remove pods by holding the stem with one hand and pulling down on the pods with the other. Select pods that have just become firm and where the beans aren't showing as bulges.

A BROAD BEAN BROAD IN THE BEAN

Origin and Varieties

There is an excellent chance that broad beans are in the top five ancient, native vegetables. They have been a part of our diet for millennia, though the original beans would have been considerably smaller.

There are different types of broad bean: Spanish or Seville, Longpod (the majority) and Windsor. Of more interest is the fact that you can have hardy types (sow in autumn) and maincrop (sow in spring). With the former, variations on a variety called 'Aquadulce' are perhaps the most useful, because they avoid the worst pests and diseases, particularly blackfly, as well as giving an early crop. However, very harsh winters can set them back.

'Crimson Flowered' broad beans are extremely attractive but generally have lower yields.

For autumn sowing use 'Aquadulce'. 'The Sutton' is a dwarf type best sown in spring and 'Express' is a reliable maincrop, too.

Pests and Diseases

Blackfly, birds, chocolate spot.

Comments

The broad bean doesn't quite win the universal plaudits that accompany, say, peas – something to do with the toughness or slight bitterness of the skin, perhaps. But then this might be more our fault than the poor bean's. If we leave them on the plant too long then what can we expect; the grey starchy beans come out of the pod like miniature, leather footballs filled with plaster of Paris. A week earlier and you'd have had tender, sweet gems.

You can remove the skins of older beans either during a meal (if you don't mind everything else going cold), or after cooking, to make a pâté. Apparently, if the scar on the bottom of the bean (the hilum, botany fans) is black, then it is overripe.

Another popular procedure is to harvest the immature pods and cook them whole like mangetout peas. Personally, I would rather eat my slippers (a not altogether dissimilar texture), but then I am just an uncouth clod who has trouble accepting a broad bean as anything other than a fat, green seed removed from a fur-lined pod.

The recommendation of pinching out the growing tip of plants when in full flower, is to remove the exact bit that is attractive to blackfly. Unfortunately, spring-sown plants often aren't big enough to do this when the blackfly moves in. Anyway, it is suggested that this succulent young growth can be used like spinach; this is second only in repulsiveness to eating the young pods. Nevertheless, it would be a shame to waste an edible plant part, so lose it in a stew. Nutrition of this leafy green morsel will be marginally higher if the blackfly have already found it.

Being a native, broad beans grow in, and prefer, cooler conditions with good levels of moisture from flowering onwards, just like all of the beans. In fact, they grow poorly in hot summer weather, being more prone to fungal diseases.

The structure of the broad bean is not the best of designs. The plants can become floppy and fall over. For this reason, especially on an exposed site, it is best to use sturdy, dwarf varieties planted in a block, or sow in a zig-zag band with a wide gap before another band. This allows a stake-and-string structure to support them. On the positive side, they require few additional nutrients, because they manufacture their own nitrogen compounds (with a little help from bacteria) and can be ready in the 'hungry gap' (May/June) to provide a good source of protein. If there is a glut, broad beans freeze well.

Also, should one plant fail, its neighbours often branch to fill the gap. Jolly decent of them.

Beans, French

Phaseolus vulgaris

(*Phaseolus,* from Greek *phaselos* for a different kind of bean; *vulgaris,* common)

Family: PAPILIONACEAE

Sowing

When: Dwarf: monthly from April to July;
Climbing: April and June

Where: Modules/cells. Later sowings can be direct.

How: One seed per cell. Direct: 4cm (1.5ins) deep. Minimum temperature of 10°C.

Transplanting

DWARF FRENCH BEANS AND THE CURSE OF LOW HANGING PODS

When: Approximately five weeks after sowing; end of May for first sowing.

Where: Dwarf – prepared bed or containers. Climbing – prepared area with framework in place.

How: Dwarf: 20cm (8ins) apart in each direction. Climbing: rows 60cm (2ft), plants/seeds 15cm (6ins).

Fertility: Low requirement

Harvest: Pick carefully to avoid breaking stems. The pods are ready when they snap when bent, usually at around 10-20cm (4-8ins). Flat-podded varieties can be picked when they are even longer; they may have seeds bulging and still be just right. Regular picking keeps the plants producing.

Origin and Varieties

Both dwarf and climbing beans arrived in Europe in the 16th century from Central and South America – those evil Conquistadores again. They have been cultivated in Peru for over 10,000 years, apparently.

Dwarf varieties: 'Tendergreen' and 'Royalty' (purple) provide good yields and flavour.

With climbing varieties, highest yields are from flat-podded types like 'Hunter' (why does a bean get called 'Hunter'?). Most of us (well, me anyway) prefer pencil pods like 'Cobra'. Coloured varieties look terrific though need plenty of sun to 'colour up' and they tend to be lower yielding e.g. 'Blauhilde' (purple). 'Borlotto Ligua di Fuoco' (the last bit means 'firetongue') – sometimes called 'Barlotto'– which have red-splashed pods, can be found as dwarf or climbing and can be used as pods, fresh beans or dried beans.

Pests and Diseases

Blackfly, slugs, various soil-borne diseases.

Comments

They come from the Americas, so we call them French beans. Sounds like a bit of a swiz. Maybe if something arrives via another country then that is ok, like Dutch elm disease.

Anyway, French beans have the constitution of runner beans, meaning we must avoid frosts. Like peas they have wide variation with a good range of short and tall types and can be grown to harvest the pods all at once, which in a large-scale commercial operation makes automation and picking easier because it is more convenient to re-sow repeatedly than to spend time individually picking ripe pods. The opposite is true for us: it is often harder to raise and establish new crops (or to remember to do it) and we like to repeat pick from the same plants. Closer spacing of dwarf types will give the highest yields of all, but regular picking is easier with plants set wider apart. To obtain at least six weeks cropping from just one sowing, try growing climbing French beans. They are better at twining up tipis than runners, which can outgrow such a framework. However, they don't crop for as long, so two sowings may be necessary to cover all of the summer.

French beans seem more sophisticated than grumpy broad beans, that produce huge seeds in little grey leather jackets, or rampant runners producing small wooden cricket bats at the drop of a hat. Also, French beans are self-fertile: not earth-shattering news perhaps, but this means pods will be produced in conditions where there are few insects (polytunnels) or in weather that restricts insect-pollination. Runner beans sulk in extremes: too cold and there are few pollinators, too hot and the flowers won't set.

Actually, an exciting piece of information to do with the self-fertile bit is if you keep a few dried beans and sow them the following year you'll get the exact same variety. No crossing with other varieties. You'll never have to buy a packet of seeds again.

The many varieties of French bean offer a great range of possibilities. Most will produce edible pods – that's what we tend to expect – but with many you can pod them and eat fresh shelled beans (called flageolets), as with broad beans. Also, plenty of them will produce dried beans (called haricots) and there you have your storable protein. There are some terrific varieties specifically used for drying such as the Yin yang bean (with interlocking white and red-brown patches), 'Coco' (with a speckled coat) and the Cranberry bean (large dark red seeds, ideal for a stew). Let the pods dry on the plants for as long as possible: too long and the pods will start to split and drop the seeds. Continue to dry them under cover and the test of fully dry (and therefore time to stick them in a jam jar) is when you press a fingernail into the coat and it doesn't leave a mark.

A big advantage of growing climbers instead of dwarf types is that, in a wet summer, the pods are out of the reach of passing molluscs (aka slugs and snails); on short plants the ends are often vandalised at soil level. Blackfly (a black greenfly, if you see what I mean) can be a nuisance; try brushing or washing them off rather than spraying them with chemicals.

The number and range of soil-borne diseases means that it is important to be strict with your rotation: at least four years even though most of them aren't devastating.

As for support systems, feed, water, etc. use the same as for peas and runner beans; just supply them using a French accent.

Beans, Runner

Phaseolus coccineus
(*Phaseolus,* from Greek *phaselos* for a different kind of bean; *coccineus*, scarlet)
Family: PAPILIONACEAE

Sowing

When: April/early May; late May if direct sown.
Where: Pots or large modules/cells inside, or direct.
How: Half fill the containers. Place one seed in each and fill up with compost.

Transplanting

When: End of May

A DRIED POD AND EXTREMELY COLOURFUL BEAN

Where: Prepared beds with support framework.
How: Spacing of 30cm (12ins) between plants and canes. Rows 60cm (2ft) apart, or a tipi of 90cm (3ft) diameter (see facing page).
Fertility: Low requirement, though some seaweed meal would help.
Harvest: When the pods are fully grown (actual size depends on the variety) but before beans show as swellings. Regular harvesting (removing all pods that have ripened, even over-ripened) is important to keep the plants producing.

Origin and Varieties

Runner beans are originally from Mexico; wild forms were used there over 9,000 years ago. They have had a slightly bizarre time in the UK. They were introduced here in the early 17th century and four varieties are on a seed list of 1633. A century later there is a record of them being cooked, but it is odd that they were still used as ornamental climbers until late Victorian times, only then achieving widespread use as a vegetable.

Many other countries are still at the ornamental stage, leaving the runner bean vegetable as a peculiarly British (and Central American) thing. Runner beans seem to do particularly well in the English climate, circumstances permitting. One of the original four varieties is still available and worth growing: 'Painted Lady'. Other stalwarts are 'Enorma' and 'Scarlet Emperor'. 'Hestia' is an odd dwarf thing used in containers.

Pests and Diseases

Blackfly, slugs, grey mould, halo blight.

Comments

Is there anything more traditional on the allotment than a row of runner beans? Is there anything more horticulturally amusing than the support framework at the end of the season? Take a stroll around a site in September and view the results. We have the 'Moderately Inebriated' – canes all leaning at the same odd angle. There is the 'Whale Carcass' with canes sticking out at all angles like giant ribs. Then we have the 'What Runner Beans?' – a heap of plants and sticks at or around ground level.

The strongest structure is the tipi with eight or so 2.5m (8ft) canes in a circle (or an octagon for the less mathematically-challenged of you). The canes are bunched and tied together as high as you can reach. However, this is not so good for the plants, or for you when it comes to picking, with much of the growth concentrated towards that rather crowded point at the top.

The other alternative is two rows of canes leaning into the centre of the bed –

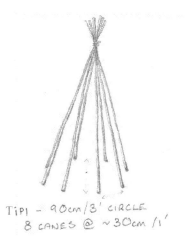

TiPi – 90cm/3' CIRCLE
8 CANES @ ~30cm /1'

HAZEL POLES, ANTI-CLOCKWISE
RUNNERS AND ONE HAVING A
LIE DOWN

an A-frame. This is the traditional structure and one that is easiest for picking, but most prone to damage. Cross-bracing or guy-ropes can strengthen it. Best of all, it avoids the 'tipi-congestion' syndrome.

The next argument is how much feeding these plants need. Many books recommend creating an open trench early in the year and piling in any waste like weeds, peelings – in fact anything you'd compost.

Don't do it. All of that material should be on a heap, which is subsequently used for plants that need the fertility. We are confusing fertility with moisture and it is the latter that the peas and beans need. On a heavy soil there is usually plenty of moisture, though it should still be improved with organic matter applied to a previous crop. On a light soil, the trench (if you use one) could be filled with newspaper and hard-to-compost items like brassica stalks. If you don't like trenches, use a thick mulch of leaf mould; water lots when flowering starts.

Next dilemma: spacing. The distances given are for the convenience of picking and watering. Half of the plant distances i.e. 15cm (6ins) gives the highest yield (and don't think you can get around it by putting two plants at 30cm (12ins)). If you wish to use the closer spacing (and also economise on canes), fit a horizontal cane along the row at ground level, then run strings from it to the ridge cane between the uprights. In other words, you alternate strings and canes at 15cm (6ins).

If you are planting out beans that have been started indoors, remember to plant under the angle of the cane and train the top around the cane in an anticlockwise direction (looking from above). They will unwind themselves if you do it clockwise.

Now here's an interesting bit. Some clever people have been crossing runner beans with French beans, which doesn't really sound all that exciting, especially since the results look pretty much like runner beans. But here's why: the new hybrids have slightly fleshier pods, a smoother skin and are not as coarse as runners and, best of all, they are self-fertile like the French beans. That means you can collect some seed at the end of the season and next year it will produce plants true to the parent, i.e. the original hybrid. Self-fertility also helps when a plant has particular issues surrounding pollination, which indeed runner beans do. Bumblebees may be in short supply at the right time, and unless you happen to have a pet hummingbird (the other main pollinator in Central America) the unpollinated flowers drop, equalling no pods. The new hybrids breeze through the problem, though I'd like to be reassured that bees will still be able to feed from the hybrid flowers. Hopefully, too, the new plants will have French bean blood in them enough to make the plants tolerate hot, dry conditions when, again, the flowers of runners can drop off. 'Firestorm' is a red hybrid and 'Moonlight' is a white-flowered hybrid.

To conclude on a controversial note: instead of bamboo canes shipped from China, leaving pandas short of a square meal, perhaps we should be using home-produced hazel poles or the like. To discuss.

Beetroot

Beta vulgaris (*Beta*, Latin name for beet; *vulgaris,* common)
Family: AMARANTHACEAE

Sowing

When: March for early crops. April – June for maincrops. Repeat sow at least 3 times for a long   supply of fresh roots.

Where: Direct into a prepared seedbed.

Containers: modules can be used (see overleaf).

How: Sow about 1-1.5cm (½in) deep. Earlies: space rows 15cm (6ins) apart; thin seedlings to 15cm (6ins).

Maincrop: space rows 30cm (12ins) apart; thin seedlings to 2.5cm (1in). *Fertility* Medium requirement.

Harvest Clear rows as required, or selectively pull from within the row to leave the remainder to continue growing. Early varieties tend to be harvested smaller (about table tennis ball size).

Time of sowing to harvest is two to three months.

Store in the ground with some protection (soil, fleece, straw or all three); or lift and keep in a cool, humid environment (e.g. a box of damp sand).

SLIGHTLY NIBBLED PROBLEM - FREE BEETROOT

Origin and Varieties

The ancestor of the beetroot was pretty widespread: from the UK to Asia. Called maritime/wild sea beet, it also gave rise to sugar beet, mangolds and chard. Used initially as a medicine and a leaf vegetable, the round purple root wasn't developed until the 16th century; until then the root was little more than a dull carrot. The Russians and Eastern Europeans really went for beetroot, with lots of recipes dating back to the 18th Century (e.g. borscht); but it wasn't until the Victorians got their hands on it that it was widely grown here.

'Boltardy' is a very reliable variety especially with early sowings. Another old variety is 'Detroit Globe'. 'Forono' has a short cylindrical root with great flavour, though not for early sowings. 'Monogram' and 'Moneta' are monogerm varieties.

Pests and Diseases

Birds can pull out seedlings, blackfly (the same one that goes for beans), slugs.

Comments

For what is really a rather easy vegetable to grow, beetroot is quite underplanted. It might be historical; 50 years ago, it seems it was only ever eaten pickled from a jar.

It is easy to grow, mainly because it requires only moderate fertility and it's not number one on a slug's menu.

Pickled beetroot is rather splendid, of course, and is an excellent way of preserving. We are perhaps more adventurous nowadays; the simplest and most nutritionally rewarding uses being grating it into salads or juicing. Raw beetroot and its juice have been shown to contain high levels of antioxidants, to reduce inflammation and cell wear ant tear as well as being anti-cancer. It contains nitrates which have blood pressure-reducing properties, apparently acting within an hour of consumption. There's also tryptophan which relaxes the mind and gives a feeling of well-being; it's in chocolate, too. Perhaps go for a sense of utter joy by consuming chocolate-coated beetroot.

Is it a 'superfood' or just like other vegetables and fruit, all beneficial in their different ways?

Of mild interest is the fact that the seed you get from a packet of beetroot is actually a fruit, botanically-speaking. Not very gripping so far. However, like many fruits there is often more than one seed inside. So, is it a problem if you get more than one seedling coming up at a single point? It is if you want evenly-spaced roots, but beetroot is one of those curious vegetables that, like onions, respond well to having a number of seedlings clustered together, to the point that it is deliberately done commercially. Four or five 'seeds' are sown in cells then transplanted out without thinning, using a fairly wide spacing (30cm x 30cm). The population of roots is probably the same as if you sowed direct in lines and thinned to a uniform spacing.

Anyway, the result is an easy-to-weed row of clumps, producing a good yield of medium-sized roots; do any of us really want giant red footballs which take several light years and the output of half a power station to cook?

If this heretical talk of clusters is too scary for you, stick with the spacing given overleaf and indulge in a little light thinning of seedlings (try using narrow scissors) or use a variety like 'Monogram' that has only one seed per fruit in the first place (monogerm).

So, to summarise: fairly pest- and disease-free, extremely healthy to eat, easy to grow and storable. Well, that's all pretty positive. There just has to be a downside. Here it is:

For some people, beetroot can 'over stimulate' the digestive process, making for a somewhat active system; plus, when you 'go', the output can have an alarming purple-red colour. Be prepared. No need to go and see a gastroenterologist.

Broccoli, Purple Sprouting

Brassica oleracea Italica group
(*Brassica* – Latin for cabbages; *oleracea* – of the garden; Italica – of Italy)
Family: BRASSICACEAE

Sowing

When: May

Where: In modules/cells, trays or in a nursery seedbed.

How: In each cell sow two seeds 1cm (½in) deep; thin to one plant on emergence. In a seedbed sow in rows 15cm (6ins) apart and thin seedlings to 2.5cm (1in).

A BROCCOLI SEEDLING SHOWING 2 TRUE LEAVES AND 2 HEART-SHAPED SEED LEAVES.

Transplanting

When: June/July

Where: Final position in a prepared bed.

How: Transplant deeply – up to the seed leaves (the first leaves to appear on germination). Space 100cm (3ft) apart in each direction.

Fertility: High

Harvest: Break off the flowering shoots when you see colour, but before each little head starts to soften and individual buds separate. Remove shoots that have gone too far to keep the plant cropping. The first shoot to pick is the large central one. As picking continues, the shoots will gradually get smaller and smaller until it's not worth continuing.

Origin and Varieties

Purple sprouting broccoli, which is a winter plant, has the same origin as calabrese (a summer/autumn vegetable), namely the Middle East. Apparently, it arrived in this country relatively recently: the 18th century, which is a slight surprise since the Romans were thrilled by the stuff and they usually took their crops with them wherever they went.

The main varieties of purple sprouting broccoli produce in the new year, the exact months depending on the location and the variety. For example, an early crop in a favourable location could be produced in January using 'Purple Sprouting Early'; or as late as May in a different situation using, say, 'Purple Sprouting Late'. For more interesting names than these try 'Rudolph' and 'Cardinal', respectively.

There are white versions which tend to crop later and more lightly, though they perhaps have a superior flavour.

Pests and Diseases

Slugs (when plants are small), grey/mealy aphids, cabbage white butterfly caterpillars, pigeons.

Comments

What a wonderful vegetable. A tasty superfood produced at a fairly dull time of year, certainly in terms of the range of produce available.

It contains many different antioxidants, protecting against a range of cancers – or so we are told. In 100g there is 150% of your RDA (recommended daily allowance) of vitamin C. There is vitamin A, some B-complexes and K, as well as a great range of minerals like iron, calcium and zinc. The flower heads even have some Omega-3 fatty acids, which must be good news, mustn't it?

Just don't overcook it. How about a light steaming, with some lemon juice, black pepper and tamari added?

Purple sprouting broccoli is often known as PSB by those lazy slugabeds who can't be bothered to give it its full name. Anyway, PSB is in the ground for a long time, and has a wide spacing. The resulting plants are amongst the biggest we grow, at over a metre (3-4ft) tall.

This gives us an opportunity. When the plants are still small, the gaps in between can be filled with a quick crop of lettuce, radish or even turnips. This is known as intercropping and uses land that would otherwise be a home for weeds. As long as the growth of the PSB is not affected, this is fine. When intercrops have been removed, a green manure can be sown to cover the soil and improve it. The PSB should be big enough by now not to be affected and the green manure (say, clover) will still be there once the plants have been removed.

In recent years there have been varieties bred that crop before the end of the year, sometimes late summer onwards (e.g. Santee F1 sown February to May to harvest June to November). This is great because PSB is a little easier to grow than calabrese, which would be ready around the same time. However, it is as a late winter crop that it comes into its own.

There is also a white broccoli that lasts from year to year ('9 Star Perennial') as long as it is repeatedly picked to stop it flowering fully. Even so, it can run out of steam after a few years.

By far the worst nuisance for PSB is pigeons, which, as well as sitting on the tops of the plant pecking it to bits, don't seem to be inclined to control their toiletry habits. Netting raised above the plants is the best bet, though a trifle inconvenient when weeding, picking etc.

Brussels Sprouts

Brassica oleracea Gemmifera Group (*Brassica*, classical Latin for the cabbage tribe; *oleracea*, of the vegetable garden; Gemmifera – bearing gems)

Family: BRASSICACEAE

Sowing

When: March to April

Where: Seed trays, modules or a nursery seedbed.

How: Compost/soil temperatures should be about 10°C (50°F) for strong, rapid germination. See page 114 for sowing techniques.

Transplanting

When: May/June (approx. six weeks after sowing)

Where: Prepared bed outside (rotation with cabbages).

How: 60-75cm (2-2½ft) in all directions depending on size of variety. Plant 'firmly' and deeply (up to the lower leaves).

A SPROUT PLANT WITH HOLE-MAKERS

Fertility: High requirement.

Harvest: September to March depending on variety. Remove buttons from the bottom of the stalk as the leaves die off. Use the top 'cabbage' as required (usually close to the end of button harvesting). Removal in late September will, however, speed up the development of buttons in a very early crop.

Origin and Varieties

The Brussels sprout, a variant of the cabbage, was discovered in Belgium in the late 18th century. There were few varieties for many years and the original plants had a long growing season (sometimes the seed was sown at the end of the previous year) and were tall – up to 1.5m (5ft) high.

Cultivars now range from 75cm to 120cm (2½-4ft) and have different maturing times. For example, the old variety 'Early Half Tall' (the name is a bit of a giveaway) produces buttons on short plants from September to November. It is an 'open-pollinated' type, meaning the sprouts gradually develop up the stem. Another example is 'Doric F1', a vigorous plant producing from December to February. It is an F1 hybrid meaning that, if required, the sprouts could be picked all in one go – they mature on the stalk simultaneously.

Select a variety that will produce sprouts at your chosen time. There are many varieties with different flavours. Trial and error may be the best approach here to find the one to suit you. A good example is the variety 'Diablo F1', which was described in a national taste test as having a flavour 'somewhat akin to silage'. Yet it is still there in the catalogues – so somebody must like it....

Pests and Diseases

Pigeons, slugs and snails, cabbage white butterfly, cabbage root fly, clubroot, mildew, grey aphids.

Comments

Ah, the evil Brussels sprout. Hunched malevolently in a corner of the vegetable patch until its moment comes at the festive period and it can be unleashed to wreak havoc on the nation's digestive systems. Is there a vegetable grown so widely yet so popularly despised? Shame really; it's only a mutant cabbage with edible buds, after all. It also has exceptionally good levels of vitamins and minerals (vitamin C, iron and calcium, for example).

Perhaps the reputation is down to the cooking and with a little imagination it could be redeemed. How about shredding them and sautéing with garlic, orange juice and black pepper? Strewth – that's not very Christmassy. Surely, we must do the traditional thing and boil them whole until they are barely-held-together balls of mush? Actually, try steaming instead of boiling them. In that way you will avoid that ghastly smell reminiscent of the workhouse, not to mention the inferior taste.

There is something odd about the Brussels sprout. Occasionally, the sprouts themselves develop loosely, or 'blow'; not those tight, shiny ping-pong-ball-sized (if you're lucky) buds but miniature loose-leaf lettuces. If you were expecting the former, this will be disappointing. If you're not bothered by the latter then there's no problem, especially since there is now a cross between Brussels and kale which are intended to produce little rosettes that don't look that different to blown sprouts.

Let us assume you actually wanted the round things. What causes the blowing? Depends who you ask.

Some will say the soil is not firm enough, or more pertinently that the plants are rocking around. Well, it's hard to see how that creates blown sprouts, but plant them deeper, earth-up, put a stick next to them or do all of these, just in case. On a heavy soil it is not easy to push down a hefty wellie, firmly either side of a new Brussels sprout plant and feel good about it. That's compaction; so easy…

Another reason is too much feeding; to be specific nitrogen. Well, this is another poser, because all of the leafy brassicas need good levels of nitrogen. Perhaps apply your nutrients in the best form: compost again, to be on the safe side.

Too wide spacing has also been implicated, so do as you're told (previous page). A final suggestion has been F1 hybrids or rather the opposite, open-pollinated types. Without spending the rest of this book rambling aimlessly about the pros and cons of F1's, not to mention what it all means, the two main features, as far as Brussels sprouts are concerned, are: cost (F1 hybrid seeds are more expensive);

and as mentioned under varieties, the sprouts are all ready to pick at the same time. Also, you *might* get fewer blown sprouts…

Like most of the brassicas, especially the big leafy Western ones, Brussels are subject to the deadly triad of slugs / snails, cabbage white butterfly and pigeons. Any one of these can reduce a substantial plant to tatters.
Well, we've got remedies for all of these (see p.159 onwards) but here are a couple of extras for the latter two.
Cabbage white butterflies are desperate to access your plants so will try to sneak under or through any netting. If you left a plant outside the netting they will be very happy to lay their eggs on that and not trouble the others. You then stroll up and concentrate your attentions on that plant, rubbing off the yellow eggs. It's a nice theory.
Pigeons will peck through bird netting unless it is raised up off the plants. In other words, you have to build a structure or use supports. Simply using canes topped off with plant pots or plastic bottles to stop the canes going through the net is not bad but when you need to access the plants for picking, weeding, etc. it all gets a little messy. The pots fall off, the canes get caught and you are lucky if you escape without being trussed up like a fly in a web. Try growing a tall variety of Brussels sprouts - space the plants throughout all the other winter brassicas and you have in-built supports. The heads of the Brussels plants will get pecked of course, but you'll still get a harvest of sprouts, albeit slightly reduced. See, there is a silver lining to everything.

Cabbages

Brassica oleracea Capitata group
(*Brassica*, Latin for cabbage or Celtic (*bresic*) for cabbage; *oleracea*, of
the garden; Capitata – having a head)
Family: BRASSICACEAE

Sowing

When: Spring cabbage: July/August. Summer
cabbage: February to March. Winter cabbage:
May

Where: In modules (cells) or trays. For large
quantities, try sowing in a nursery seedbed/
coldframe.

How: Modules: two seeds per cell; thin to one.
Seedbed: sow in drills (rows) 15cm (6ins) apart,
then thin to one plant every 2.5cm (1in).

A CABBAGE UNDER
THREAT

Transplanting:

When: When there are two true leaves (not the
little heart-shaped seed leaves); harden off and then plant out.

Where: Prepared bed.

How: Spring: 30cm (12ins) apart in all directions. Summer: 35-45cm (1418ins)
apart in all directions; closer spacing gives a high yield of slightly smaller heads.
Autumn: 45cm (18ins) apart in all directions.

Fertility: High requirement.

Harvest: As appropriate, when the heads are fully formed, but before splitting.
Cut off and leave the stump to form loose leaves for a second harvest.

Origin and Varieties

Brassica oleracea is the wild cabbage and a native of much of Europe, including
the UK. This may be why the Celtic word for cabbage, *bresic*, is said to be the
origin of the word 'brassica'. Cabbages with heads (which the wild cabbage
doesn't possess) have been developed over the centuries, from way before the
Romans to the present day. The white cabbage was produced in the 9th century
and the equally weighty red cabbage was developed soon afterwards.

Favourites for spring cabbage include 'Pixie' and 'Wintergreen'; for summer
cabbages try 'Greyhound' (pointed) or 'Golden Acre' (round), and for winter
there is the ever-wonderful 'January King'. 'Pixie' is quite versatile in that it can
be sown a number of times in the year to provide leaves almost all year round.

Pests and Diseases

Pigeons, slugs and snails, cabbage white butterfly, mildew, cabbage root fly,
clubroot, grey aphid.

26

Comments

A vital vegetable, an essential esculent, cabbage is probably the subject of most 'you must eat your greens' demands, to which the reply should be 'I'd love to if you hadn't boiled them to death'.

I suspect there is a deodorant spray used in many institutions; not pine or lemon, but boiled cabbage. The malodorous sulphur-ness is a symptom of over-cooking. 'Tis a bit sad, for this versatile plant is relatively easy to grow and it is possible to harvest a version of it all year round. Careful cooking to preserve the goodness and flavour is important: a dark green, leafy cabbage, as opposed to the heavy white things, for example, will give almost two thirds of your daily vitamin C requirement per 100g. Some will be lost in cooking.

Other benefits include lots of antioxidants (particularly in red cabbage), B vitamins and the minerals iron, potassium, magnesium and manganese. The uses of cabbage medicinally have been universally praised, including the Romans using it for centuries for every disease. There are one or two dissenters: Robert Burton (17thC) said it 'sends up black vapours to the brain'. Well, if it was over-cooked, it's not surprising depression set in – ask generations of school children.

Although the best cabbages, nutritionally-speaking, are the looser dark green ones, there are a number of splendid attributes of the white (and red) cabbage. These include the little squeaky noise when it is cut, the fantastic patterns inside, like curls of smoke, and, of course, the making of superbly-nutritious sauerkraut.

The first decision is: when do you want your cabbage? This will dictate which group your cabbage is in, and hence the sowing time. For example, if you were desirous of nutrient-packed, succulent leaves in May (I'm trying not to be too biased here), one way would be to sow spring cabbage the previous year.

Spring greens consist of loose leaves cut young. It is possible to sow spring cabbage seeds direct in the ground in say July, thin to 10cm (4ins) apart, and then the following spring remove the spring greens for an early crop and leave the remaining plants at a spacing of 30cm (12ins) to 'head up' as spring cabbage. There were a lot of 'springs' there – I hope you were concentrating. To get all-year-round cabbages you will need to select varieties and sowing times from each of those categories on the previous page, as well as checking the different maturing times from sowing to harvest. On top of that, some varieties last quite a while ('stand well') once the head has formed, while others 'go over' quite rapidly. Select carefully.

The mantra for leafy vegetables is 'nitrogen and water', and cabbages need plenty of both. However, don't forget that the minerals and vitamins that cabbages provide you with originate from the soil, so supply a good range of all nutrients, along with the nitrogen. Compost'll sort you out.

27

Calabrese
(See also Broccoli)

Brassica oleracea Italica group
(*Brassica*, Latin for cabbage; *oleracea*, of the garden; Italica – of Italy)
Family: BRASSICACEAE

Sowing
When: March and April to early June
Where: March, sowing in modules indoors;
later sowings can be direct.
How: Modules: two seeds per module/cell.
Direct sowings: two to three seeds at intervals
of 15cm (6ins) in rows 30cm (12ins) apart. Thin
to one plant in both cases.

Transplanting
When: Module-raised plants can be planted out
about a month after sowing, e.g. April from a
March sowing.

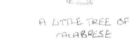

A LITTLE TREE OF
CALABRESE

Where: Prepared bed outside (rotation with cabbages).
How: Space transplants 15cm (6ins) apart with 30cm (12ins) between rows.
Fertility: High requirement.
Harvest: Cut the large head at the top when the individual buds are visible, yet
still tight together. The plant dictates when you can do this, but it is generally
about four months after sowing. Break off side shoots as they develop and use
in the kitchen.

Origin and Varieties
Sometimes called green sprouting broccoli, summer or Italian broccoli, the word
calabrese signifies its origins more accurately. It's from the bottom of Italy, the
bit of the boot kicking Sicily, called Calabria.

Technically, it's incorrect to call this Broccoli, though everyone does. It's better
known than the purple or white, winter sprouting broccoli, mainly through its
popularity abroad (and subsequent imports).

In a way, it is a shame not to call it broccoli, since the word means branch or arm
(Latin *brachium*) and it is well suited to this: a miniature tree with stout branches
and dense foliage.

Most of the varieties available are hybrids producing large heads. Cheaper – and
you get more seed as well – is the non-hybrid (open-pollinated) variety 'Green
Sprouting' giving lots of side shoots.

Often listed as a variety of calabrese (in this book, included under cauliflower) is Romanesco with its exotic-looking, pointed, dense, lime-green head.

Pests and Diseases

Pigeons, slugs and snails, cabbage root fly, cabbage white butterfly, club root, mildew, grey aphids.

Comments

What we are eating is the unopened flower head – a huge one, at that. 'Unopened' is a key word – we should harvest when the buds are clearly visible yet still firm and certainly not showing any colour. The calabrese you buy, a great grey-green plastic-coated thing, is the terminal head; the one at the top of the plant, that is first to appear.

When you grow it you can choose between varieties that will do their best to provide you with one of these big heads, or have a smaller terminal head followed by repeated production of side shoots, as you do with purple sprouting broccoli. A wider spacing of plants will also encourage the formation of side shoots.

Calabrese is an independent little plant. It will be a little grumpy if you disturb its roots, hence it is not wise to start it in a seedbed. However, it will fill the space you give it (wider or closer spacings than those shown give a similar yield) and will continue to produce side shoots for weeks, well into the autumn. Decent sort of chap.

Very close spacing gives most of the yield from small terminal heads; the overall yield for that patch being the same as if you used wider spacings, which produces a lot more side shoots. It is perhaps worthwhile doing the latter to provide a gradual production.

Looking after your calabrese plants is an exercise in moderation. Fertility, generally, is high for brassicas, though a medium level is actually fine for calabrese. Watering is not as vital as say, beans, but they still mustn't dry out, and weeding is important, early on particularly: but because of the spacing and good leaf cover it's less of an issue later.

It would be untoward to talk about calabrese without mentioning its properties. It is, as they say, up there when it comes to nutrition, along with its relative, sprouting broccoli. In fact, it sits neatly in that wretched category 'Superfood'. There are good levels of protein (4.3g/100g fresh weight), enough vitamin C in 100g of cooked (44mg) or uncooked (79mg) broccoli to cover your recommended daily dose (40mg) and good levels of other vitamins and minerals including calcium and iron. On top of that, there's lots of fibre and antioxidants. As always, such figures depend on your personal requirements, where and how the plants have been grown and how they have been prepared to eat. Perhaps just grow your own organically and don't worry about it.

Carrots

Daucus carota

(*Daucus,* from Greek for carrot; *carota,* from Latin for carrot)

Family: APIACEAE

Sowing

When: March to June.

Where: Direct into a prepared seedbed, with loosened soil.

How: Rows should be 15cm (6ins) apart for the highest yield of medium sized carrots. With early sowings: thin to 10cm (4ins). Maincrop/later sowings: thin to 3cm (1½ins). Few people follow this row spacing because there is a higher percentage of rejects (too small); this is despite getting the greatest weight per unit area. Also it is harder to weed between the rows. More common is a row spacing of 30cm (12ins) (providing fewer rejects, larger roots and a lower total yield).

A CASUAL CARROT

Fertility: Medium requirement.

Harvest: Selectively pull young carrots when they reach a usable size (judge from the diameter of the top of the carrot – if it is visible). Harvest maincrop carrots by inserting a fork alongside the row and tilting just enough to loosen the roots, then lift out. Maincrop carrots can be left in the ground in cold weather if they are insulated by, say, laying down straw or garden fleece. If they freeze, they develop miniature cracks and then rot. When left in the ground, they are more vulnerable to slugs and continued attack by the notorious carrot root fly, so it is common to lift all of the roots and store them in damp sand in a frost-free, cool place.

Origin and Varieties

Carrot ancestry has been well documented. The first 'domesticated' carrot was purple and originated in the Afghanistan area: it is known as the Eastern carrot. The Western carrot is different in a number of ways, including root and foliage colour, though it is thought to have been derived from the Eastern carrot.

There were red, yellow and white versions available in the UK from the 15th century onwards, the orange type being selected in Holland in the 16-17th century. Some varieties still survive from then but more popular varieties, that also still exist, were developed in France in the 19th century.

Early carrots can be grown from 'Amsterdam Forcing'. Next comes

'Early Nantes' and 'Chantenay Red Cored' and then the wonderful maincrop 'Autumn King'

Pests and Diseases
Carrot root fly, slugs, aphids, various root rots.

Comments
What a great scientific name: 'carrot carrot'.

Nothing seems to typify success in vegetable growing as a good carrot crop. To gardeners with a heavy/clayey soil, any carrots at all are the holy grail. In reality, it is not so much the soil as what comes with it that makes for a good yield of carrots. Typically, heavy soils are wet soils and that means slugs. Often the seed has actually germinated but the seed leaves have been grazed off, maybe all in one night. Consequently, we think they haven't come up at all.

If slugs are kept at bay, carrots can still grow well in a soil with a lot of clay. However, it is easier for them to grow in a lighter soil, so the addition of organic matter to a vegetable garden on a regular basis will help enormously. It is said that a stony soil will make carrots fork (or fang) – in other words, produce more than one root to create shapes to titillate those of us deprived of more conventional amusements. Actually, stones have little effect if the carrot can grow and push them out of the way. Stony, clay soil is, therefore, to be avoided – or improved (see above). It is also said that fresh organic matter incorporated into the soil has a similar naughty effect. If you wish to add organic matter of any sort simply apply it as a mulch when they are a few weeks old.

Perhaps another way of looking at forked carrots is, 'what is the worry?' They taste the same and if you're not selling them in a supermarket, the only problem is cleaning them. Not too dreadful a prospect, I hope.

If you wanted to make your carrots look even more disturbing, then you could spend valuable time whittling away with a knife to get rid of the carrot root fly damage. The tunnels created by the grub (larva) of this pest are fairly superficial depending on the severity of attack, but it allows rot to get in. Hence, this is particularly an issue if you are storing carrots, in the ground especially.

Stopping carrot root fly typifies organic growing almost more than any other pest. Chemically, pesticides are used that are absorbed into the skin of the root. This means that, to avoid the residues, you should peel your non-organic carrot, so removing the most nutritious part in the process.

Organic solutions: Cover with fleece; use resistant varieties; sow maincrop carrots after the peak onslaught of carrot root fly (early June), or interplant with rows of onions to mask the carrot smell. Good luck.

Cauliflower

Brassica oleracea Botrytis group
(*Brassica*, Latin for cabbage or Celtic (*bresic*) for cabbage; *oleracea*, of the garden;
Botrytis – like a bunch of grapes)
Family: BRASSICACEAE

Sowing

When: For curds ready June-July, sow in October or January. For curds ready August to November, sow March to May. For curds ready December to May sow early May to early June.
Where: Unless large numbers are required, use modules (cells).
How: Two seeds per cell, thinning to one seedling. Transplant into pots if necessary to prevent any check to growth.

A 'BRAIN'
OF CAULIFLOWER

Transplanting

When: When transplants have about 3 true leaves.
Where: Prepared bed (rotation with cabbages).
How: Spacing is widest for the winter crops (75cm (2½ft)) and narrowest for those ready in mid-summer (50cm (20ins)). Use 68cm (27ins) spacing for autumn crops, or if you get fed up with all of this, just use 60cm (2ft) for everything.
Mini cauliflowers can be produced using larger varieties like 'Snowball' but with very close spacing of 15cm (6ins).
Fertility: High requirement (but see 'Comments')
Harvest: Cut when you can see a formed head ('curd') – you may need to part the leaves to check.

Origin and Varieties

Along with Brussels sprouts, kale and cabbage itself, cauliflower originated from the wild cabbage, *Brassica oleracea*, which is found all over the place. Caulis apparently were a distinct type of brassica over 2500 years ago in the Eastern Mediterranean. The Romans were partial, as ever, to a bit of cauliflower. The fact that it took until the 16th century for the cauli to move from Italy to France (and then on to the UK in the 17th century) suggests that later types were developed that were more interesting, and their movements were consequently worthy of noting; either that or the roads between Italy and France were really rubbish for about 1600 years.

Many and varied are the varieties available. 'All Year Round' is an all-purpose white cauliflower used at different times of year to give a succession of heads.

'Snowball' is another favourite with a number of sowings and smaller white heads if spaced more closely. 'Purple Cape' is an overwintering variety ready in early spring with a strong purple head. 'Sunset F1' is a summer variety with a slightly disturbing orange head, a bit like a white one that's past it. Choose varieties for successional cropping. 'Idol' (if you can find it) is a 'designer' mini cauli. Romanesco cauliflower varieties are limited: try 'Veronica' or 'Cello'.

Pests and Diseases

Slugs and snails, cabbage white butterfly, mildew, cabbage root fly, clubroot, grey aphid, pigeons.

Comments

Old Latin for cabbage (and stem) is 'cauli' and that has given rise to a number of different plant names, not least cauliflower, therefore meaning cabbage flower. It has been transformed into the word 'cole' and that is found in different words like collards (loose leaf brassicas such as spring greens), kohlrabi, coleslaw and even kale.

The cauliflower head, or curd, is a pretty bizarre structure. It forms from a bud that will eventually develop into a flower but, unlike calabrese which is the flower in bud, the cauliflower curd is modified and thickened flower parts. If left, the flowers as we recognise them – petals, reproductive parts – emerge from this head.

There are a number of different types, reflecting the country of development. Many vegetables undergo this process and to say that X vegetable was introduced into Y country in Z year is only half the story. They are being developed all the time with new forms going backwards and forwards. In the case of cauliflowers, we have a range of varieties from different places allowing us to grow them all year round. Alternatively, use 'All Year Round'. Cauliflower seems to show up the nasty side of brassicas as well as any of them.

Overcooking not only releases the nutritionally-important sulphur compounds to give that overwhelming 'boiled cabbage' smell, but also destroys vitamins. If there is one thing caulis have it is vitamin C – enough in a 100g helping to fulfil your Recommended Daily Allowance. Unfortunately, boiling gets rid of about half this; steaming and stir-frying preserves considerably more, not to mention making the cauli infinitely more edible.

Included in this group, (though sometimes counted as Italian broccoli / calabrese), is the type Romanesco. This has an unusual and rather beautiful head: lime green in colour. They are well worth a closeup examination: small, pointed buds spiral around a pyramid, like the top of a highly ornate minaret (a Fibonacci fractal, maths fans). Not content with that, Romanesco has a vaguely mealy texture, definitely more like cauliflower than calabrese, but still with a lovely flavour. They're usually ready to harvest in late summer to mid-autumn.

The little pointed bits easily get damaged in commercial production, so your home-grown heads have the advantage. Hurrah.

Concerning the growing of cauliflowers, here is some specialist advice: Don't. Maybe that was just prejudiced advice rather than specialist: I find it harder to grow a good specimen of cauliflower than any other vegetable. All manner of sizes and deformities have appeared on my plot, whilst the experts in Cornwall and East Anglia have trouble stopping huge creamy-white footballs from bursting out of the earth.

Let us try to sort out the secrets of my incompetence – where did it all go wrong? Firstly, ensure that there is no check to growth right from the transplant stage – plant out (or pot on) without delay. Next, the plants need steady levels of moisture, so good watering is essential: this is the reason for the range of spacings given, i.e. wider equals less water stress. Misting is even recommended on summer crops to keep the plants cool and unstressed; caulis prefer cooler conditions. Good levels of nutrients in the soil are required, as with all brassicas, but don't overdo it: too much nitrogen in particular can give soft, frost-susceptible growth.

There we are – we'll all have no trouble from now on.

Celeriac

Apium graveolens var *rapaceum*
(*Apium,* from the Celtic *apon* meaning water;
graveolens, heavily scented; *rapaceum,* turnip-like)
Family: APIACEAE

Sowing

When: March

Where: Indoors, in modules (cells) or trays.

How: The seed is very small and needs light to germinate, so it should be barely covered. Put in two or three seeds per cell and thin to one later. Place in a plastic bag to stop the surface (and seed) from drying out. Germination and early growth is slow.

Transplanting

When: End of May

Where: Prepared beds, outdoors (rotation with carrots).

How: Transplant seedlings after hardening off at a spacing of about 30cm (12ins) in all directions.

Fertility: Medium requirement.

Harvest: A lot of growth takes place late in the season so harvesting would be in September at the earliest. Dig out of the ground or cut out using a knife. In areas with a mild climate (or with lots of protection) celeriac can be left in the ground over winter.

Origin and Varieties

This is a very close relative of celery (often called 'turnip-rooted celery') that has been popular in Europe for a long time and, despite being introduced into the UK about 300 years ago, has remained a somewhat obscure vegetable here. Gardening books frequently omitted it even 30 years ago, though it got a glowing report in *Gardens Illustrated* magazine in 1880.

Few varieties are available, the most common being 'Giant Prague' and 'Prinz', both names giving a clue to celeriac's origins.

Pests and Diseases

Carrot root fly, slugs.

Comments

I was in two minds whether to include celeriac, this being a book of common vegetables. It is not commonly grown but is here purely because it ought to be, and I'm in charge.

It's tastier than the turnip and easier than celery, and though it is not without its challenges, you usually get something at the end, be it thumbnail, fist or head-sized. To keep to the body parts theme, you'd usually hope for a root the size of a knee (well, my knee anyway; I have perfect celeriac-sized knees). Celeriac needs a long growing season, which is fine. Start it early, in March. More of a problem is when you come to transplant it. At this time, it is at its most sensitive to low temperatures and we have to get it adjusted to going outside; by 'sensitive' I mean that the plant will bolt (go to seed) before it forms its big root. Hopefully, the seasons are behaving themselves and it has all warmed up. If not, there is nothing to stop you potting them up and keeping them ticking over until conditions have improved.

Pests and diseases aren't really a major problem: slugs in the early stages and carrot root fly (since celeriac is in the same family as carrots) are the worst. The aim during the summer is maintaining steady levels of moisture and nutrients. If the soil is a bit poor, then it can be improved with a mulch of compost between plants, shortly after transplanting. If the soil is already in good heart, use leaf mould.

When harvesting, I find it easiest to cut the root out of the ground using a big old kitchen knife. In the process, this removes some of the small, culinarily useless roots that make it extremely hard to pull out, which is helpful – the rear end of a celeriac looks like a bag of worms. It is not worth trying to clean it up by washing – cut it off.

Pull off the battered, tough outer leaves then cut the central young punk tuft to save for flavouring. It is good practice with root vegetables to remove the leaves at harvest, particularly if the roots aren't used straight away. Either that or put the whole thing in a plastic bag in the fridge. The first thing I do with a lovely handful of bunched carrots with great mounds of soft, fresh foliage exploding out of the tops, is to take the lot off and compost it.

What you do with the root is now up to you. Being of limited culinary imagination, I tend to use it grated in salads with carrot and beetroot, or put it in soups and stews. Fortunately (for everyone) this isn't a cookbook, so try a few things out yourself.

Celery

Apium graveolens

(*Apium*, from the Celtic *apon*, meaning water; *graveolens* means heavily scented)
Family: APIACEAE

Sowing

When: April

Where: Modules/cells

How: Sow two or three seeds on the surface of the
compost. Don't cover with more compost. Keep
the modules out of direct sunlight with a clear
lid/plastic bag covering them. Thin to one seedling.

Transplanting

When: May/June

Where: Well-prepared bed outside (rotation with
carrots).

How: Only transplant when it is warm outside. Use
a spacing of no more than 30cm (12ins) in each
direction. This gives good yields of blanched stalks.
Closer planting will give higher yields overall but
smaller, narrower stalks.

NON-SELF BLANCHING CELERY
IMPRISONED FOR NOT BEING
WHITE ENOUGH

Fertility: Medium requirement.

Harvest: Harvesting is in the region of four months after sowing, which, with an
April sowing, gives only a short period when the celery is at its peak and before
frosts, especially in the north. Heads can be stored in a cool, frost free place.

Origin and Varieties

Native to Europe and Asia (that's pretty widespread, then) wild celery likes
moist places: ditches, damp meadows, marshy bits. The cultivated variety,
sometimes known as *Apium graveolens* var. *dulce* – the last word meaning
'sweet'– was developed in 17th Century Italy.

What is interesting about this is that at some point in the past someone saw the
potential in this stringy, bitter bog plant to persevere with cultivation and
selection to get something approaching modern-day 'sweet' celery. Obviously
one of those brief lulls in history when we weren't spending all of our time
killing each other. Or perhaps a series of lulls; it's not a quick process.
For ease of growing try 'Golden Self Blanching' or 'Green Utah'.

Pests and Diseases

Slugs, celery fly, celery leaf spot, carrot root fly.

Comments

Just think, if the celery hadn't fattened up along the whole length of its leaf stalks and it was just the bottoms that were succulent, it would be a 'bulb' like onions or fennel.

Let's look at something interesting: one of the best things about celery is that each stalk forms a long wide groove. This can be filled with tasty things like peanut butter (crunchy, no salt).

It is said that to eat celery you use more energy digesting it than is available from it: the ultimate slimming food. Certainly, it is questionable whether the amount of effort required to grow it is returned in joy and appreciation of the end product.

Celery and celeriac are quite unusual in vegetable circles in that they need light to germinate (hence the sowing on the compost surface). This is a sensible mechanism: these are tiny seeds and have low resources. If I was a celery seed, I would want to know that I was near or at the surface because I couldn't grow very far after germinating. Indeed, if I was a celery seed, life would be considerably simpler altogether.

Also, like celeriac, celery is sensitive to low temperatures when it is at the stage to transplant and will flower prematurely if it is less than 10° C throughout the night, so it is not worth starting too early.

It needs lots of moisture – no surprise there, when it consists of so much water – and it is exceptionally easy to find slugs between the stalks. Celery is shallow rooting, so with regard to preventing water stress, it is the ideal candidate for a mulch.

The less fashionable type nowadays is the original blanching or trench celery, where the plants are individually wrapped (cardboard tube, sections of waste downpipe, etc.) or earthed up in lovely fen soil in order to make the stalks sweeter and white.

Then come 'self-blanching' types: it does it all by itself, helped by relatively close spacing. Finally, there are varieties of American green celery, which couldn't care less if they have white stalks: they are narrow and pale green. Blanching celery is hardiest of the lot, so should stand a little longer into autumn, though it is by far the fiddliest to grow. To make life easier try self blanching or American celery.

Chard and Leaf Beet

Beta vulgaris subsp. *cicla*
(*Beta*, Latin for beet; *vulgaris*, common)
Family: AMARANTHACEAE

Sowing

DELIGHTFULLY BUBBLY
LEAF OF RHUBARB CHARD

When: Twice a year: March/April and
July/August

Where: Usually, directly sown.

How: Rows should be 40cm (15ins) apart. Seed
can be sown along the drills and thinned to 30cm
(12ins), or a couple of seeds sown every 30cm
(12ins) then thinned to one plant at each 'station'.

Fertility: Medium requirement (rotation with
beetroot). Larger types may need extra feed.

Harvest: Selectively pick leaves as required from
a variety of plants (such as Swiss and Rhubarb
chards), or clear-cut plants, working your way
along a row. It would be splendid if, by the time
you finish a row, the plants at the other end have regrown and you can start
again. When clear-cutting with a large knife (watch your fingers) at about 3cm
(1in), it's worth sorting the leaves there and then, placing yellowing, spotty or
very damaged leaves in the compost and popping the remainder straight into a
plastic bag.

Origin and Varieties

This is an old Mediterranean vegetable, probably from Sicily, where all parts
were eaten, including the roots. There are many different forms of chard, all
providing a long-lasting supply of leaves and stalks.

The 'Swiss' part of the name was apparently introduced by seed catalogues to
distinguish the plant from true spinach, which was considered to be French. To
confuse matters, the 'chard' bit is from the French *carde* which compares this
plant to the cardoon, a large specimen grown for its edible leaf stalks.

Swiss chard has few varieties, 'Fordhook Giant' being an old favourite. The
slightly more refined Rhubarb chard has several versions, the main difference
being the pinky-red colour of the stem. Rainbow chard is a mixture of colours;
try 'Bright Lights'. Perpetual spinach, aka leaf beet, is smaller still and green:
'Erbette' has proved to be a reliable variety.

Pests and Diseases

Slugs (not too bad), mildew

Comments

A combination of convenience, lack of space and a lack of patience has thrust a number of related, yet distinct plants into this section. They are grown, harvested and even used in much the same way and, of course, it helps that they are all the same species. Let's sort them out:

Swiss Chard (Silver or Seakale beet) is the giant of the group. It has huge, bubbly leaves, vaguely like the surface of a dark green mattress. Some people may say it tastes quite similar too, but this would be slander. You almost get two vegetables in one, with the broad, thick, white stalks thrown in. The leaf and stalk are usually separated and cooked, if not in different dishes, then at different times.

Ruby/Rhubarb/Rainbow Chard still has big leaves, but the stalks are narrower and usually coloured. The lovely rainbow chard has a mix of colours, the stalks and leaf veins being pink, purple, orange, yellow, white etc.

Perpetual spinach/Leaf beet/Spinach beet, unlike the coloured chard, where there are distinct differences between them, are all the same thing. Make up another combination of names if you like: 'perpetual leaf'? Anyway, this type is marginally less attractive than the previous chards, being smaller with pale green stalks and mid-green leaves shaped a little like a goose's foot. This is no coincidence, since the old name for this whole family is Goosefoot. It is closer in appearance and usage to true spinach.

The chards have excellent levels of nutrients, on a par with true spinach (Vitamins A, B, C and K and minerals, especially iron). They also happen to be a lot easier to grow, with two sowings a year. With repeated cutting/ picking it is theoretically possible to have chard leaves all year round, depending on the severity of the winter. If it is quite harsh, the plants die back, but will re-shoot in the spring. Another advantage over true spinach is its ability to withstand hot summer weather.

An unfortunate feature it shares with true spinach is the content of oxalic acid (see spinach).

The tops of beetroot are exactly the same as chard and can happily be eaten, though they tend to get a bit shabby by root-harvesting time.

This whole group is remarkably trouble-free. Yes, slugs may have a go at your veg, but chard and beetroot will often remain untouched. Snails make holes in the leaves and mildew can occur, especially if you are less diligent with the watering than required. Water at the plants' bases to stop them getting stressed; at the same time keeping the leaves dry.

Corn Salad/Lamb's Lettuce

Valerianella locusta
(*Valerianella*, from Latin, *valeo*, to be healthy; *locusta*: obscure origin)
Family: VALERIANACEAE

Sowing

When: August to September.
Where: Direct into a prepared bed or between existing plants with wide gaps in between.
How: Sow thinly in rows 15cm (6ins) apart. Thin to 10cm (4ins) between plants.
Fertility: Low requirement.
Harvest: Remove individual leaves or, more commonly, take out whole plants when they are big enough. Harvest from October all through the winter until the plants start to flower in the spring.

HARDY, TASTY, HEALTHY, FIDDLY...

Origin and Varieties

Corn salad is a native plant and has been 'foraged' by European peasants for centuries. Well, this peasant now sows his own. Most countries in Europe have their own name for it, reflecting its enduring use. We have at least two names for it in the UK, Corn Salad referring to its appearance amongst cereals and Lamb's Lettuce because, apparently, sheep like it. Wise animals. Not to be outdone, the French have two names as well: Mache, which is now quite widespread, and the usefully descriptive, Doucette – Little Soft One.
The Germans call it Feldsalat, which even I can translate as Field Salad. There's a reasonable range of varieties for such an underused vegetable. The one most commonly encountered is 'Vit', a vigorous plant that can be sown throughout the year, which also has some mildew resistance. A variety with 'an excellent flavour' is 'Verte de Cambrai', though it also has smaller leaves.

Pests and Diseases

Slugs (minimal damage), powdery mildew.

Comments

What a versatile little plant is the corn salad; it can be a nutritious winter vegetable, a weed or a green manure. It doesn't succeed terribly well as either of the last two because it is so easy to hoe away that other tougher weeds like couch grass will laugh their socks off at it. As a green manure it can give reasonable coverage of the soil, especially over winter, but contributes little in the way of organic matter.
This leaves its function as a vegetable and in the winter it comes into its own.

41

Totally hardy, it can be grown amongst other plants (intercropping) or just given its own space. Interestingly, it is the reverse of other winter salads, by doing more poorly under cover; without excellent ventilation it readily gets powdery mildew. Rocket, mizuna, mustards, etc. do better with winter protection and the older they are the hotter they get. Sweet little corn salad stays the same, with soft, mild-flavoured leaves, only going off the rails a bit when it starts to flower.

Flowering takes place in spring, when light and temperature is increasing. You have the choice of composting the remaining plants – chopping them into the soil *a la* green manure – or leaving them to set seed. If the latter, then you will have a good coverage of plants later in the year and, again, you can deal with them as and when you like. Corn salad is that rarity – a useful self-seeding vegetable. More good news: it has great levels of vitamins, especially C (three times that of lettuce) at a time of year when we need every vitamin we can get hold of.

So what's wrong with it? There must be something, because hardy lettuces have largely taken its place in the repertoire of winter salads.

Well, it appears that size *does* matter. Corn salad is a small plant and is fiddly both with picking and preparing leaves: they rarely reach 15cm (6ins), and usually half that. Some people pick leaves individually, but depending on how many plants you have, it's often easier to remove the whole thing. You then have to separate the leaves in a bowl of water to get the soil off. You can grow corn salad at other times of year, but beware that it can go to seed relatively rapidly in hot weather, unlike lettuce.

Claytonia/Winter Purslane/Miner's Lettuce
(*Claytonia perfoliata*)

There is just enough space to squeeze in a bit about claytonia, which, apart from being right next to corn salad in catalogues, is very like it in a number of ways. It is not quite as hardy, but has the same spacing, cultivation and good levels of vitamin C. It has little shovel-shaped fleshy leaves on the end of thin stalks, with a delicate flavour. It is now naturalised in this country, having journeyed from the States, where the reverse has happened with corn salad. The name 'miner's lettuce' refers to the use made of it by hairy, Bourbon-drinking prospectors in California, panning for gold and trying to avoid scurvy by eating claytonia.

Courgettes

Cucurbita pepo

(*Cucurbita,* Latin for gourd; *pepo,* probably from Greek *pepon* or sun-baked)

Family: CUCURBITACEAE

Sowing

When: April

Where: Small pots or modules

How: Sow one seed on its edge per cell. Keep warm: 20°C would be ideal.

Transplanting

When: End of May (South) Early June (North)

Where: Outside in a prepared bed (rotation with squash).

How: Space out plants about 75cm (2½ft) in each direction. On a 1.2m (4ft) wide bed you end up with a zig-zag. Place compost in the planting hole

Fertility: High requirement.

Harvest: Cut, or carefully twist off fruit when about 15cm (6ins) long. Picking ensures continued production.

AN OVERWEIGHT COURGETTE – SOMETIMES CALLED A MARROW

Origin and Varieties

Courgettes originated in Central America as a type of squash. Squash and its relations have been cultivated for thousands of years in the Americas and arrived in Europe during the 16th century. It was developed in Italy three centuries later, as the more recognisable courgette we have today.

The word courgette is French for 'little squash or gourd'; Zucchini is Italian for the same thing and is the name used in the USA. For many years they were known over here as Baby Marrows, which is pretty much what they were. In the UK, we seem to have taken ages to get used to them: they've been here for years but only within the last 40 years have they got remotely popular.

There are many new F1 hybrid varieties, giving strong, even crops of uniform fruit. There are also plenty of old types still going well, like 'Nero di Milano', 'Black Beauty', 'All Green Bush' and the bright yellow 'Gold Rush'.

Pests and Diseases

Slugs and snails, powdery mildew, cucumber mosaic virus.

Comments

Oh for goodness sake. Look, how many courgettes do you actually want? Nothing else approaches runner beans for the 'Glut of the Year' award.

There's a story in New England of people being reminded to lock their cars – apparently folk had been breaking into them and then running off, leaving behind a mound of courgettes. What I like about that is the fact that when we get a glut we're loathe to just compost it, to the point that we might force other people to take the surplus.

There are groups in this country that will take any donated vegetables, to make soup or redistribute them, etc. Alternatively, there may be a chance to sell produce; though to avoid the limited nature of a stall at your local farmers' market being stocked only with courgettes, try growing too much of other things.

Courgettes are not the most exciting vegetable nutrition-wise, containing some Vitamin A, potassium and manganese, but they bulk out many a recipe, being essential in favourites like ratatouille.

They're pretty easy to grow; pander to their requirements and it will all go swimmingly: warmth, moisture and a high fertility. For the former, don't plant out too early (wait until the frosts are supposed to have finished) plus put in an order for a jolly pleasant British summer. Moisture and nutrients are provided by compost at planting, and as a mulch. Additional watering is likely if you get the summer you wish for.

To make life more interesting, you might like to try training your courgette plants up a (very stout) stake. A 1.5m (5') stake should do it and as the plant grows tie it loosely against the stake so as not to crush the hollow stem. The value of doing this, apart from keeping you off the streets, is the fruit is cleaner and, most importantly, further out of the reach of slugs. When watering, it is easier to keep the majority of the leaves dry (= less mildew) and apparently the plants crop for longer. Beware: some varieties are better at growing upwards in a straight line than others and you may need to remove any side branches if they form.

Feeling slightly poetical, the life of a courgette plant could, with a small stretch of the imagination, be likened to our own humble existence: we both start off needing cosseting – keeping warm and protected. We then set off into the world, or allotment, and are strong and vigorous, at the peak of our reproductive powers. Towards the end of our 'seasons', the days don't have the same length as they used to. We become tired and less productive. Ailments begin to affect us. The pooped courgette plant gets powdery mildew all over towards the end. Occasionally there is an attack earlier in the life of the plant, but it often copes, just as we do when younger. Not that we get powdery mildew, you understand. I wish I hadn't started that, now…

Cucumbers

Cucumis sativus

(*Cucumis* – Latin for cucumber; *sativus* – cultivated)

Family: CUCURBITACEAE

Sowing

When: April

Where: Indoors, in small pots or modules/cells.

How: One seed, inserted on its edge, per container.

Transplanting

When: Late May

Where: In well-prepared ground outside or in
containers. (rotation with squash and courgettes).

How: Plant with compost in each hole and add a
mulch of the same after planting. Space the plants
about 90cm (3ft) apart. On a 1.2m (4ft) bed, plant
in a zigzag, effectively in two lines about 60cm
(2ft) apart.

A SHORT, SLIGHTLY
PRICKLY BUT STILL RATHER
LOVELY CUCUMBER

Fertility: High requirement.

Harvest: When the fruit is 'full' and dark green (presuming they are supposed
to be that colour). Overripe fruit are fat (a kind of middle-age spread), and
yellowed. Keep picking to stimulate further production.

Origins and Varieties

Cucumbers, the original wild version, come from India and have been in
cultivation for over 3000 years. Like many plants with such a history, they have
changed over the years with selection and breeding. For many years they
produced small, dark green fruits that were prickly and quite bitter. As a result,
they were usually cooked.

The cucumbers we eat in this country are very narrow in range: mainly long,
green cylinders in plastic coats, from the supermarket. The ones we grow can be
more varied though.

There are two types of cucumbers, resembling the cordon (indoor) and bush
types (outdoor) of tomatoes: they are Frame cucumbers, grown mainly inside up
strings or canes, and Ridge cucumbers, grown outside as bushy, spreading
plants, with a little protection, if possible.

Frame cucumbers concern us less here, but if you have a very favourable,
sheltered position it might be worth trying them like a cordon tomato. Really
they are for greenhouses/polytunnels.

Instead of 'Ridge' cucumbers perhaps we ought simply to say 'Outdoor'.

45

'Marketmore' produces short fruit (about 20cm (8ins)) with a few spines and 'Sonja' is smoother and a little longer at 25cm (10ins). Both are traditional Ridge types and free of bitterness. 'Crystal Lemon' has a curious round, yellow fruit, about 10cm (4ins) across, sometimes with quite a thick skin. Also gherkins, mini warty cucumbers for pickling, can be planted outdoors. Try 'Hokus' which has a 10cm (4ins) fruit.

Pests and Diseases

Cucumber mosaic virus, powdery mildew, grey mould, slugs and snails.

Comments

The first question you might ask is, 'why grow cucumbers?' – an awkward, scrambling plant that produces potentially bitter, nutrition-free fruit. Composed mainly of water, cucumbers are a great slimming aid with a high vitamin to calorie ratio. This doesn't mean it has many vitamins, just very few calories. The vitamins and minerals they contain are all less than 5% of RDA (per 100g), with the exception of Vitamin K, and are mainly in the skin. The skin will house the bitterness too (if it has it) as well as the pesticides, when chemically grown.

None of this is very positive but it would be a disappointing world without cucumbers, the moisture added to a dry sandwich and ballast to a mixed salad being two good examples. Where would the Famous Five be without 'cucumber sandwiches and lashings of ginger beer'? What would we do without amusing pictures of mum lying down with slices of cucumber over her eyes?

Ridge cucumbers are so called because they have traditionally been grown by digging out a trench, putting in plenty of compost, and then covering with the soil, forming a ridge. This isn't necessary (though it would presumably give good results). It does, however, indicate the preferred soil conditions: water and nutrients readily available, with good drainage.

Despite being outdoor cucumbers, they will perform much better if they are given shelter and warmth. This could be the location you grow them or the protection you provide: windbreaks around beds, sheltered by other crops or cloches.

Sowing can be done directly outside, but trying to protect and maintain a little seedling is far more difficult than starting off the plants inside.

There is a particular technical bit to follow with outdoor cukes: when the stems have produced about six leaves, pinch out the tip above the sixth one. As with most pruning, this stimulates the buds below to break and sideshoots to form. These can be left to scramble up some support or spread over the ground.

With outdoor cucumbers you don't have the concern of whether to remove male flowers or not, which might be the case with Frame/Indoor types. For that reason, you don't need to buy expensive 'all female' varieties, unless of course you insist on seedless fruit. What's wrong with a few seeds, I say?

Fennel

Foeniculum vulgare var. *azoricum*

(*Foeniculum*, derived from Latin for hay; v*ulgare*, common; *azoricum*, from the Azores) Family: APIACEAE

Sowing

When: April to July
Where: Preferably in modules/cells. Can be directly sown.
How: Two seeds per cell; thin to one seedling. Direct – sow thinly in rows at least 30cm (12ins) apart and thin to about 30cm(12ins).

A 'HAND' OF FENNEL

Transplanting

When: When the soil is warm, from May onwards.
Where: Prepared ground (rotation with carrots).
How: Space at a minimum of 30cm (12ins) in each direction.
Fertility: Medium requirement. Mulch after planting.
Harvest: Ready about three months after sowing when the size of a cricket ball. Cut off the bulb above soil level to leave the stump behind. Eat within a week.

Origin and Varieties

Fennel, in its herb form, has been grown for its seeds and leaves since who knows when (a long time). Not so our fat little Florence fennel, which was apparently developed from the herb in Italy in the 17th century. It was included in a London nurseryman's seed list in the 18th century. The origin of the common name comes from the USA when seed was sent from the American consul in Florence to Thomas Jefferson in 1824.

Florence fennel didn't really become popular in the UK (or the States) until the second half of the 20th century, and it still has a struggle.

'Finale' is a large, flattened type, whilst 'Fino' and 'Romanesco' have more typical rounded bulbs.

Pests and Diseases

Slugs

Comments

There's a wide range of vitamins and minerals in fennel but it doesn't have a surfeit of any of them; it is quite often suggested as a substitute for celery in recipes. Nevertheless, mixed with other vegetables it makes a contribution to our nutrition intake.

Its strong point is the fresh, crisp, mild-aniseed swollen leaf bases (making it, botanically, a bulb). When the flavour is at its best, it is a great addition to a salad. When cooked, it becomes less 'aniseedy'.

The foliage is fine and feathery, like a parsnip with a bad hair day, and can be used as well as the bulb, in salads etc.

Because Florence fennel doesn't like root disturbance and will revolt if given a check to its growth (e.g. too cold, early on), the most successful approaches are to raise it indoors in individual containers and plant into a warm soil; or sow directly into that warm soil. Because of slug issues, I favour the former. A revolting fennel really means one that produces a flower stem too soon – correctly known as bolting. If it happens very early, the plant will be useless. If it happens later, the flower stalk can be removed as soon as possible and the bulb, such as it is, used straight away.

It is interesting, especially with the lack of pests and diseases, that fennel's main issue is this problem of bolting. But then, if you think about it, it is not so surprising. For centuries fennel, in its herb form, has been bred for the rapid production of seed. With Florence fennel, which, as mentioned, has been derived from the herb, we are trying to undo this, so that it grows and lasts as a vegetable.

Most varieties available now are termed 'bolt resistant', but this is relative. Apart from getting upset at having its roots fiddled with, or from being too chilly early on, it will also be grumpy if you don't keep moisture levels steady. Apparently, its preferred native environment is warm and moist; a bit too dry and up pops the flower stalk. A mulch after planting will help keep water in the soil.

Don't forget the added bonuses of growing fennel (actually, to be able to forget them you have to have known them in the first place, and I haven't told you yet, sorry): if it bolts and it doesn't look like you can use any of the bulb, let it flower and harvest the seed for fennel tea.

After harvesting a bulb, the root plus stump is left in the ground, which will reshoot to provide young sprouts that can be used in the same way as the bulb. The mature plant is fairly cold tolerant, so it will survive into the autumn quite well, though not the winter, without deterioration.

Garlic

Allium sativum
(*Allium*, Latin for garlic; *sativum*, cultivated)
Family: ALLIACEAE

Planting

When: October to February.

Where: Directly into the ground (rotation with onions).

How: Break up a bulb into individual cloves. You will get 150 - 250 cloves per Kg of bulbs – cloves vary hugely in size even within the bulb. Part the soil with a trowel and ease in the clove so that the tip still shows. Use a spacing of 15cm (6ins) in all directions.

Fertility: Medium requirement; particularly potassium (see 'Fertility').

Harvest: Harvest straight away once the tops start falling over. If you leave it too long, the bulbs' skin splits and it opens up, possibly falling apart; then the tops disappear and you can't find the bulb. Dry off for two weeks then store in a cool and dry place.

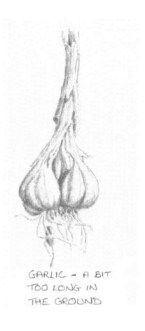

GARLIC - A BIT
TOO LONG IN
THE GROUND

Origin and Varieties

Originally from central Asia, bulb garlic has taken a long time to get anywhere in this country, which is odd seeing as wild garlic, whose fragrance can often be scented in the woods, is native to our shores. It's been around in Europe for millennia and its importance is reflected in the use of its classical name for the whole family. Meanwhile, in the UK we only recently got around to using any quantity of it. Elizabeth David, the great cookery writer speaks of having to go to a little Italian shop in Soho to find it in the 1950s. I have a vegetable book from about 35 years ago which has a sentence under 'garlic' (in the herb section, incidentally): 'Used in large quantities on the continent but not a major feature of the British diet.' There are two types of garlic:

Hardneck: flower stalks form at the same time as the bulb and show as a hard dry stalk sticking up the middle of bought bulbs. They have perhaps got the best flavour and are maybe easier to peel e.g. 'Edenrose'.

Softneck: no flower stalk (usually). Most commercial garlic is softneck. Bulbs last longer in store and have more cloves per bulb (though are possibly smaller) e.g. 'Solent Wight'.

Pests and Diseases

White rot, rust.

Comments

The qualities of garlic are well-documented: anti-asthmatic, anti-fungal, antibacterial, anti-social... Personally, I'm far less bothered by somebody smelling of garlic than of some synthetic perfumes. For me, it's not really anti-social, just different-smelling.

Buy a variety of 'seed' garlic (a clean bulb sold for propagation) that is adapted to your conditions. Save a few cloves from one year to plant the next (as long as you've not noticed any pests or diseases) and so save yourself money on seed garlic. Greengrocer-bought bulbs may be from foreign parts and so may not be suitable for us.

For such a sun-loving little individual, garlic needs one to two months of low temperatures to initiate bulb development. For this reason, it is planted before the end of February. Select a variety to fit in with your planting time: e.g. 'Vallelado' is for autumn planting, while the cleverly-named 'Flavour' is for late winter planting, presumably not requiring quite as much cold.

Going back to hardneck and softneck types (see previous page), to confuse matters, softnecks can occasionally produce a flower stalk. Flower shoots should be removed from any bulbs to concentrate resources into clove growth.

However, we have stumbled upon another delicacy apart from the bulb. The flower stalk or more correctly 'scape' can be cut young (before it is big enough to go curly) and cooked in stir fries. Some folk grow garlic purely for the scape. There are three main ways of growing (and harvesting) garlic:

1.   Green garlic – when you break up a bulb into individual cloves ready to plant, keep the smallest (usually found in the middle) and plant them 2.5cm (1in) apart in rows 15cm (6ins) apart, like spring onions. Harvest in May for lovely, sweet garlic compensating for the fact that your stored garlic just ran out.

2.   Wet garlic – large cloves planted as normal are harvested after bulb formation but while the leaves are still green. This is particularly juicy.

3.   Dry garlic – As for wet but wait until the tops start to fall over before lifting, drying and storing.

On heavier soils and in wet seasons, bulb size is smaller, partly because the fungus brown rust on the leaves restricts growth. Wider spacing is sometimes recommended but the only sure-fire way is keeping the leaves dry. Polytunnel or ventilated cloches, anybody?

Rust aside, it's all plain sailing; oh yes, apart from white rot, basal rot, botrytis rot, viruses, eelworm, onion fly and thrips. I am mongering a scare. White rot can be an issue, but generally you'll be fine.

Kale

Brassica oleacea Acephela group
(*Brassica*, Latin for cabbage; *oleracea*, of the garden; Acephela – headless)
Family: BRASSICACEAE

Sowing

When: May

Where: In modules/cells or in a nursery seedbed/coldframe.

How: Sow two seeds per cell and thin to one seedling. In a seedbed, sow thinly in 15cm (6ins) rows and thin to one plant every 2.5cm (1ins). This is worth doing if you need lots of plants.

Transplanting

When: July

Where: Prepared bed (rotation with cabbage family).

D.G.C. KALE – USEFUL PERCH

How: Transplant kale plants 45cm (18ins) in each direction. On a 1.2m (4ft) bed you can get three staggered rows along it.

Fertility: High-ish requirement.

Harvest: Pull off lowest leaves and discard damaged or yellowing ones (see overleaf).

Origin and Varieties

Kale has been developed from the same wild cabbage as (you guessed it) cabbage, Brussels sprouts and cauliflowers. Possibly, because it is a simpler structure, some kale is as recognisable today as it was over 2000 years ago when the Greeks and Romans were playing around with different types. Kale was (and still is) used for animal feed in this country, Cut out the middle man (cow) and eat the stuff yourself.

'Dwarf Green Curled' is one of the best kales for flavour, appearance and ease of growing. There are some great red-purple versions. 'Nero di Toscano' has thick, narrow leaves of a very dark green. 'Thousand Head' is tall, plain, productive and extremely hardy.

Pests and Diseases

As for cabbages, only less so.

Comments

Why is kale such a wonderful food, nutritionally that is? It has an undeserved reputation for being difficult to make edible, though there are numerous wonderful recipes like kale crisps or sautéed kale with garlic and soy sauce. In

51

my book, it is streets ahead of most vegetables, including those in its own family. Whilst so closely related to cabbage, broccoli, etc., it is superior in vitamin content in almost every way. It's not clear whether all the different types of kale are as potent as one another, in this respect.

Let us not worry about this and just enjoy the leaves all year round.

Traditional production is for the six months over winter (October to March at least), but don't exclude it at other times. Sow earlier than recommended on the previous page for a late summer crop or repeat sow directly into the ground to clear cut young leaves for salad throughout the year.

Nearly all of vegetables prefer a sunny site and kale is no exception. It will, however, produce a reasonable crop in partial shade.

Curly kale is such odd stuff. It probably started life as a novelty, but with such densely convoluted, springy leaves you could probably make a decent mattress out of it. Maybe it baffles pigeons and snails more than other brassicas. 'Nero di Toscano' (or just black kale) is thicker and tougher, though, in the right dishes, will blow your socks off with vitamins. In fact, this is a rule of thumb: the darker green the cabbage or its relations, the more nutritious and healthy.

A third, completely different kale is 'Red Russian', probably now synonymous with 'Ragged Jack'. The leaves are flatter than the other two but with indented and wavy edges. The stalks and veins are purple and the leaf blades are blue-grey, making them jolly attractive even if the plant as a whole seems a bit messy. As with other leafy vegetables, a good range of nutrients in the soil is required, with an extra helping of nitrogen. Good homemade compost can sort this out for you. Watering is important to establish the plants, especially in a very dry spell, but because most kale is growing in autumn and winter, this is usually not an issue.

How many leaves you pick from a single plant depends on a number of factors like greed, how many plants you have, and the time it would take to produce more leaves. The last bit is affected by weather, the variety and the number of leaves you have left on. So, you could pick almost to the top in one go if you have plenty of time for them to re-grow, or take just a few leaves from each plant. The only time you remove the very top leaves is just before it starts the flowering process in spring. End of plant.

Leeks

Allium porrum
(*Allium*, classical Latin for garlic; *porrum*, classical Latin for leek)
Family: ALLIACEAE

Sowing

When: April
Where: Nursery seed bed/coldframe. Can be sown in trays or modules.
How: Sow thinly in rows 15cm (6ins) apart and thin to 2.5cm (1in). In modules, sow two seeds per cell and thin to one

Transplanting

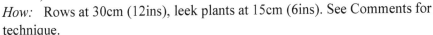

A LEEK ON A LEAN

When: June
Where: Open ground, prepared bed (rotation with onions).
How: Rows at 30cm (12ins), leek plants at 15cm (6ins). See Comments for technique.
Fertility: Medium requirement – apply nutrients if possible as compost before planting, or shortly after as a mulch.
Harvest: Either cut out of the ground or lift with a fork, starting in October. Select individual leeks, allowing the remainder to continue growing. Remove any damaged outer leaves. At the end of the season, if the ground is required for the next crop, any remaining leeks can be removed complete with roots and buried up to their necks all together in a shady place (i.e. 'heeled in').
They will store better like this than in a fridge.

Origins and Varieties

Like onions, this is a traveller from Asia Minor, possibly the Mediterranean area. It probably arrived in the UK after the Romans, in the sixth or seventh century. The adoption of the leek as a national emblem of Wales supposedly stems from the time they were attached to hats to distinguish the Welsh in battle, led by St. David or King Cadwallader (take your pick), from the evil Saxons, Either way, it was an excellent incentive to grow leeks.
A good range of varieties exist, ranging from the tall, thinner old favourite 'Musselburgh' to the short, fatter 'The Lyon'. The purple-leaved 'St. Victor' is very attractive.

Pests and Diseases

Leek moth, slugs and snails, leek rust.

Comments

Is there a more important vegetable in the history of this septic isle? The leek was one of the most valuable medieval vegetables. It provides a good range of nutrients over a long period and withstands the hardest winters.

I think the flavour is terrific and you have a choice of textures: the tougher, nutrient-rich blue-green (sometimes purple) foliage, and the sweeter, more succulent white shaft. Neither should be discarded, especially the former; yet it often is. Commercially, the tops of leeks are removed at harvest leaving a short Y-shape of green atop the white stem, probably to make it look prettier and transport more easily. We should use all of the green tops, though they may need a little extra cooking.

You wouldn't have thought so after all this time, but the raising and planting of leeks is a bit controversial. Firstly, the raising: a lot of people are addicted to containers and growing media and will start off leeks in trays or modules. This is fine, though the transplants will be smaller and more delicate.

Leeks respond very well to having their own little nursery patch outside in the soil, in a coldframe if possible. Here, they will grow in vast numbers with no cost of materials and produce transplants of a robust size: pencil thick and about 25cm (10ins) long.

Some maths for you: if it takes two men two-and-a-half days to dig 24m of ditch; sorry, wrong problem: if you want leeks for six months and you eat, say, three per week (adjust as appropriate) how many leeks do you need and how much land to grow them?

Answer: approx. 26 weeks x 3 = 78 leeks: using the spacing overleaf gives about 12m (40ft) of row or 3m (10ft) of a bed with four rows side by side. Who would have thought arithmetic could be so much fun?

Anyway, sow at least 100-150 seeds to ensure enough plants.

Next, the planting. The traditional method is very widely used and successful: thrust a dibber (often a broken spade handle with sharpened end) into the earth, twist and withdraw. Drop in a leek seedling: if raised in a seed tray it might disappear; if grown outside you might have trimmed its roots to fit it into the hole and then removed the ends of leaves to compensate for root loss.

Are you still following me?

Fill the hole with water – no soil, just water. And that's it.

A radical alternative is to part the soil with a trowel, stuff in the leek then firm and water. You don't even need to dig a hole. Result – just as successful. If it is an issue of creating as much white stem as possible, then that depends on how deep you go with your trowel or dibber.

You can always draw up soil around the stem later on ('earthing up') to improve the blanching effect.

Lettuce

Lactuca sativa

(*Lactuca*, from the Latin *lac,* milk, referring to the sap; *sativa*, cultivated)
Family: ASTERACEAE

Sowing

When: From March to October depending on
location, variety and protection.
Where: Can be sown directly into the soil or
started in trays or modules.
How: Sow thinly in rows 30cm (12ins) apart and
thin to 30cm (12ins), using the thinnings
gradually; or leave all seedlings and follow cut-
and-come-again. Sow thinly in trays or two per
cell of modules, thinning to one plant.

AN ALMOST ENTIRE
HEAD OF
COS LETTUCE

Transplanting

When: Throughout the year
Where: In gaps amongst crops (intercropping) or where one crop
has just finished and before the next is ready to go in.
How: Usually spacings of about 30cm (12ins) in all directions
Fertility: Low requirement.
Harvest: Cut whole heads (some re-growth may come from the stump) or
pick outer leaves progressively throughout the season.

Origin and Varieties

It is thought that modern-day lettuce originated from the wild prickly lettuce
Lactuca serriola that grows throughout Europe and over into Asia. The
Egyptians are credited with the first breeding programme and the Greeks have
the honour of producing a type that still has a name that reveals its origins: the
cos lettuce, from the island in the Dodecanese known as Kos. More recent times
have shown the development of lettuces with a wide range of colour, shape and
disease resistance. 'Salad Bowl' and 'Lollo Rossa' are perhaps the best known
loose-leaf types, 'Saxo' and 'Navara' (both dark red) are more recent. 'Lobjoit's
Green Cos' and 'Little Gem' (miniature) are both familiar cos types and 'Winter
Density' is a hardy semi-cos.

Pests and Diseases

Slugs, mildew, root aphids.

Comments

Where do you start with the simple lettuce? Possibly the most discarded vegetable in the world, especially if you're a burger-eater: over 90% of the salad served with burgers in the US are never eaten.

Relatively low in nutrients and high in water, what is the point, you may ask? Well, in some cases, like the wretched butterhead (with its soft, flabby yellow-green heads), or the dreadful crisphead, aka Iceberg (green-tinged water in a non-frozen solid) there isn't one – point, that is.

If you want to add freshness to a sandwich and a moderate level of interest to a leafy salad I suggest you choose a more open, loose-leaf type, or alternatively a cos with its medium-green, upright heads; there are more nutrients (and flavour) in green or purple leaves. It makes sense, therefore, to grow lettuce that doesn't have a dense head, inside of which the leaves are yellow.

Loose-leaf types like 'Lollo Rosso' or 'Salad Bowl' can be cut whole or picked a few leaves at a time. The latter method will give an overall higher yield than from one cut head, plus removing hiding places for slugs.

Lettuce is the salad leaf for late spring-summer when other ingredients like rocket and mustard don't grow so well. More accurately, lettuce 'holds' well; but in hot weather be sure to water regularly to avoid 'bolting' – going to seed. Comparatively speaking, other salads can flower before you can pick a leaf.

Lactuca species contain a substance called *lactucarium*, which has sedative and analgesic properties and has the common name of 'lettuce opium'. Indeed, the sap can be reduced by evaporation to give a smokeable solid. This is something of a shock: the simple, innocent lettuce being a narcotic? It's a little like finding your 12-year-old niece is a dealer in automatic firearms. Fortunately, the common lettuce *Lactuca sativa* produces only very small quantities of it and there would be little outcome from eating lots of lettuce other than the sedative effect of boredom.

Another helpful feature of loose-leaf types is that you can choose varieties with wavy or jagged edges. Apart from making your meal that bit more thrilling, you can't tell if a slug has had a bite or two and consequently you won't get upset.

Having had two mentions already, my homily on the lettuce continues with the slug theme, since they are arch enemy number one. It would be fair to say that to some, the lettuce is synonymous with these evil little creatures. Red lettuces are less attractive to slugs and snails than green ones. Fact. It doesn't mean that they won't get eaten, it's just that the green ones get eaten first.

Onions

Allium cepa
(*Allium*, Latin for garlic; *cepa*, Latin for onion)
Family: ALLIACEAE

Sowing (Seeds)

When: Over-wintering types: mid August (for June/ July harvest).

Maincrop types: March (for September harvest) – avoid cold, wet conditions .

Where: Direct outside.

How: Rows 25cm (10ins) apart, seeds sown thinly and thinned to 5cm (2ins) for maximum yields of medium bulbs; or to 10cm (4ins) for lower yields of larger bulbs.

A PIN-STRIPED ONION

Planting (Sets)

When: Over-wintering types – October (for June/ July harvest). Maincrop types – March/April (for September harvest).

Where: Prepared bed outside.

How: Rows 25cm (10ins) apart, sets 10cm (4ins) apart.

Fertility: Medium requirement.

Harvest: Wait until the tops have fallen over by themselves before carefully lifting out. Leave in a warm, sunny place to dry for a couple of weeks, then hang up in net bags in a cool, dry place and use as required. They could last well over six months, stored properly. An alternative to this is to plait them on a piece of (strong) string. Take about 1.2 m of string and double up to create a loop. Hang it up and tie in the first onion to the bottom. Feed further onion tops in and out of the two strands of string, building from the bottom upwards. Over-wintered onions won't store until the following year like maincrop onions.

Special note: When buying sets they are sold by weight: they weigh about 4g per set so this equates to around 250 per kilo, (or six per oz).

Origins and Varieties

Another contender for the most ancient vegetable award, the homeland of the onion is thought to be the Middle East, where they were foraged by hunter-gatherers, meaning that they were being used in prehistoric times. As a cultivated plant, the Egyptians used them over 5000 years ago. In fact the Egyptians, Greeks and Romans did all manner of things with onions, some of which involved eating them.

The Romans brought them to the UK, which, if you think about it, was the least they could do since they weren't invited. They (onions, not Romans) have been a mainstay ever since.

For autumn-planting, try 'Radar'; for maincrop onions, a couple of old favourites are 'Sturon' and 'Stuttgarter Giant'. 'Red Baron' is a lovely dark red but is prone to bolting: make sure you buy 'heat treated' sets to avoid this.

Pests and Diseases

Birds, onion fly, stem and bulb eelworm, leaf miner, downy mildew, white rot.

Comments

Looking at the internal structure of a vegetable is, I'm sure you'll agree, really quite fascinating. Instead of gawping at the television, I'll spend many an evening gazing at the insides of a parsnip. In the case of the onion, this could also be productive.

Like other bulbs, the majority of its structure is leaves – or more accurately, swollen leaf bases, making up a storage organ. When it was growing, the rings in your onion were the bottoms of the bluey-green tubular leaves. It makes sense that the more leaves it produces, the more rings your onion has, hopefully meaning a bigger bulb. All we have to do is makes sure there are plenty of leaves. No trouble.

Let us start at the beginning. Most of us, on a small scale, will plant onion sets – mini bulbs grown for us on a nursery. In other words, we start part way through the growing process. If given the choice, always go for small specimens – less than 15mm (0.6in) diameter, which will be far less likely to flower prematurely, or bolt (go to seed). If this happens, no decent bulb will be produced. Break off the flower head as soon as you see it and use what is left straight away.

On a larger, market-garden scale, five to eight seeds may be sown in each of many cells and planted out with a wide spacing (30cm (12ins) in all directions) when they look like little clumps of grass. They are left un-thinned. The result will be clusters of medium-sized bulbs. It's a technique that – key point coming up – allows easy weeding.

On our amateur scale, onion sets are close together in lines and we must spend many a happy hour keeping them weed-free. Take note of this thoroughly alarming statistic: for every day of weed competition, your onion yield will be reduced by 4%. This means that if you put off that urgent weeding for a couple of weeks, you'll have lost almost 50%. Blimey. Anyway, whether starting the onions indoors in cells or planting out sets, we are getting as many leaves on the plant as possible before it starts to form the bulb.

Your onions need moderate watering and nutrients and lots of sunshine, so choose an appropriate site – somewhere near the Mediterranean would be nice –

Nice, perhaps. In practice, you will be planting where your rotation tells you, but you get the idea, don't you?

When planting onion sets (use a trowel, don't push them in, especially on heavy soils), you are supposed to leave the gnome's hat tip sticking out. This is so that the birds can get a good grip on them when pulling them out and throwing them away, two plots down the line. I jest. However, a reasonable solution, taking into account the water, food and weed issues, is to cover the newly planted bed with a thin layer of organic matter that hides the tips.

Spring onions must have a mention. They are a selection of the 'normal' onion, chosen for their quick growth of pencil-thick stems that are included in salads. Personally, they give me more repeats than 'Dad's Army' but if you are of a hardier disposition sow every three weeks in rows 10cm (4ins) apart, aiming for seed spacing of about 2cm (1in). Don't bother thinning. They take about 12 weeks before harvest and you can overwinter a late sowing, preferably with a cloche. Spring (or salad) onions are particularly useful if you have a gap in your cropping schedule of bulbing onions.

As mentioned, many of the varieties on offer are selections of *Allium cepa*, our very same bulbing onion. In fact, if our spring onions are left a little too long, they may develop a middle-aged spread – a small bulb. There are varieties of a different species which won't produce a bulb and which are hardier: *Allium fistulosum*, versions of which are called Welsh onions or Japanese bunching onions. Unfortunately, you are never told which varieties belong to which species. Other features of the two types, together with a couple of examples include: *A. cepa* 'White Lisbon', 'Guardsman' – sweeter, less strong, *A. fistulosum* 'Feast', 'Parade' – more pungent and disease resistant.

Because they are so reliable and easy, plus the perfectly-edible tops of shop-bought specimens have been mangled or cut off, growing your own is ideal, just don't ask me to join in.

While we are loitering in the area of related alliums, perhaps we ought to glance in the direction of shallots. These are bought, planted and cared-for just as onion sets. Plant them earlier (January to March) and give a wider spacing (20cm or 8ins apart in any direction). A cluster of little bulbs should be ready to lift and dry around July or August. Roasted whole shallots can easily be the highlight of many a dull meal. I speak from experience. The versatility in the kitchen and health-supporting qualities of the onion itself are legendary. My editor told me that he loved them so much that he was thinking of writing a recipe book where each and every recipe begins with the phrase: take an onion and chop or slice it – whether it be in the starters, main course or dessert section...

Parsnips

Pastinaca sativa

(*Pastinaca*, from *pastus* meaning food; *sativa*, cultivated)

Family: APIACEAE

Sowing

When: March to May

Where: Direct into a prepared bed (rotation with carrots).

How: Sow thinly in rows 30cm (12ins) apart. Thin to 15cm (6ins). For small varieties try rows at 20cm (8ins) and thinning to about 7cm (3ins).

Fertility: Medium requirement.

Harvest: From October onwards, harvest as required. Store in the soil – they are unaffected by freezing apart from making it difficult to get them out of the ground. When new leaves appear on any remaining parsnips in the spring they will be getting woody.

MILDLY CANKERED PARSNIP

Origin and Varieties

Parsnips have been around in this country for ever: we have the wild parsnip growing widely over here. However, the large-rooted parsnip we know now, was probably originally bred in Germany, the Romans becoming quite partial to it. In the UK it has been an important vegetable for many a long year, a staple along with leeks, especially during the pre-spud era.

The sweetness of parsnips meant it was used as a sugar substitute before cane and beet were discovered, boiling down the juices to get a thick syrup.

One of the best-known parsnip varieties is 'Tender and True' and a good small variety is 'Avonresister'. Small varieties are supposed to be easier to grow in heavy soil, but all parsnips still grow well if they can get established. Lighter, deep soils are best, of course. The regular addition of organic matter will also help. If you are worried about the roots forking, then add organic matter, as a mulch, to young plants.

Pests and Diseases

Parsnip canker, carrot root fly.

Comments

I used to claim that parsnips were one of the few vegetables you wouldn't eat raw – or even cooked first – in a salad. Then a friend expressed a love for grated, raw parsnip and, despite this being a particularly daunting prospect, I have to surrender to his wisdom. Marvellous when roasted, mashed etc. Now widely used as crisps, they are also one of the few vegetables to make an excellent wine.

Home-grown parsnips are available for a long period, ensuring that come spring, they turn into wooden-cored cones, by which time you are ready for a good break. Seven to eight months of parsnips is enough for anyone and the idea of buying them in the summer, shipped halfway round the world to your wretched supermarket is, to me, frankly appalling.

They are ready, we are told, when they have received the first frost of autumn – the production of stored starches is reversed, converting them back to sugars and giving you a sweeter root in the process. The same reasoning, incidentally, for picking Brussels sprouts only after a frost. Of course, harvesting before this is also fine.

Don't listen to the packet/pundit/parsnip professional who tells you to sow parsnips in February. Even if the conditions are suitable then, there is little advantage over waiting a month or two. Germination is slow at the best of times, but in February it is painful. To mark the rows it is popular to sow quick-germinating radishes in the same drill (i.e. the little furrow in the soil). They pop up and reassure you that the parsnips will be along soon. Personally, I don't want that many radishes and I worry about radish-parsnip competition at the latter's seedling stage.

Pleasingly, parsnips are less vulnerable to slugs at all stages than most other vegetables. On a more negative note, the foliage can cause skin reactions, including the reported giant blisters on the feet of a barefoot weeder.

Another point of note with the humble parsnip is the poor viability of its seed. It often has a low germination rate and doesn't save well from year to year. In fact, it is recommended that fresh seed is bought every year – especially by the seed merchants.

Peas

Pisum sativum (*Pisum* – Latin for pea; s*ativum* – cultivated) Family:
PAPILIONACEAE

Sowing

When: From the end of March to July. Also possibly in
October/November.

Where: Direct in a prepared bed (rotation with beans).
Can also be started in modules to avoid mice.

How: In a shallow trench, 4cm (1½ins) deep, about 15cm
(6ins) wide with the seeds spaced about 10cm (4ins) apart.
Another band could be positioned 45cm (18ins) away. Or
sow in single drills, same depth, with seeds 7.5cm (3ins).

Fertility: Low requirement; though on light soils some
potassium and phosphorus could be added.

Harvest: The above spacing is for continual picking.

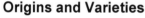

A PEA POD,
A VISITOR
AND SOME FRAS

Select pods when they are firm and full. Keep removing to ensure continued
production. Picking can start, with an earlier sowing in May (but needing
protection); but it is usually June to October.

Origins and Varieties

These things are ancient. As a species, we've been scoffing peas for getting on
10,000 years; in this country it's a more modest 2,000 (apparently, the Romans
brought them here).

Early peas were more of the mushy type: dried and then cooked in stews or
'puddings' (as in pease pudding, etc.). The big advantage was having storable
protein, especially since the majority of the population had little meat for most of
the time.

Varieties are grouped according to sowing times:

Over-wintering (smooth-seeded types) e.g. 'Feltham First', sown in the autumn
for an earlier crop the following year (they're also less sweet and lower
yielding).

First early (wrinkled seed): e.g. 'Kelvedon Wonder', quickly maturing (about
two and a half months); these follow on from the over wintering peas. Maincrop
(wrinkled seed): e.g. 'Onward', heavy yielding, taking three months to crop.
These are all dwarf, getting to about 45-75cm (18-30ins), and are repeat sown to
get a continual supply. Support is from pea sticks (try elder twigs – brittle but
branch well) or pea netting. An alternative would be my preferred option, the
longer cropping, taller growing varieties: e.g. 'Alderman' (150cm (5ft)) on a tipi.

Don't forget mangetout, sugar snap, (both sweet pods eaten whole since they lack the grisly parchment found in normal pea pods) and petit pois (very small, sweet peas).

Pests and Diseases
Birds, mice, pea moth, pea and bean weevil, mildew, fusarium wilt.

Comments
The humble pea – possibly in the same league as carrots. For some, with favourable conditions, or maybe just the knack, peas are dead easy, so what is all the fuss about? For others, so many obstacles prevent a half decent pod appearing that it makes it tempting to grab a packet of the frozen things instead. The reason: pests, mainly big ones.

Birds of a wide variety tuck in, going for the seeds when the shoots have just appeared. Having germinated, the seeds are converting stored starches into sugars making them extra attractive. Quite often you'll see a series of little pea shoots lying on the soil surface, the seed having been consumed. Next, stepping up to the serving hatch (that is a newly-sown bed of peas) are those cheery chaps, mice. The old gardeners' trick of rolling the seeds in paraffin before sowing may work; but who wants paraffin in their soil? Try Tabasco or chilli powder instead. Interestingly, only mammals detect the 'hotness' so this won't stop birds.

As an aside, it might be fun to try dusting peanuts with chilli powder before putting them in the bird feeder and seeing if squirrels can be kept away; that is unless they develop a taste for the exotic.

Meanwhile, back at the peas, a lesser nuisance is pea moth. It lays eggs at the bases of flowers leading to, oh joy, a maggot chomping away at the developing peas, carefully protected by the pod. Fortunately, only a couple of peas per pod are usually affected and it's rare to have a high percentage of pods with this little blighter rummaging around inside. Maybe the worst bit is the frass – good word, frass; drop it into casual conversation at any available opportunity – otherwise known as maggot/caterpillar/larva poop, and it makes a mess of an otherwise pristine pod. Exclusion is the best remedy (fleece), or early sowings to miss the peak population.

Like all of the bean family, commonly known as legumes, pea plants have the happy knack of joining forces with soil bacteria to accumulate valuable nitrogen in the soil. This means that you don't have to provide it. In fact, if you make too rich a soil you're wasting your precious resources; the peas will thrive, but they would have anyway.

More important is a supply of water, which should be sloshed on as soon as flowers appear, and the soil kept moist thereafter.

Potatoes, Early

Solanum tuberosum
(*Solanum*, Latin name for a related plant and assigned to potatoes; *tuberosum*,
producing tubers)
Family: SOLANACEAE

Planting

When: Mid March

Where: Directly into prepared beds.

How: Two alternatives:

1. Dig a narrow trench about 15 cm (6ins) wide
and deep, and add compost to the bottom. 'Seed'
potatoes are set about 30cm (12ins) apart and the
trenches (spaced 60cm(2') apart) filled in.

2. Nestle the seed potatoes into surface of the soil
and cover with a mound of compost (see next
page).

Maintenance – following the above alternatives
(see drawings on next page):

SLIGHTLY BLEMISHED
BUT NICELY CHITTED
EARLY POTATO

1. When the top growth reaches about 15cm (6ins) high, draw soil up around
the plant ('earthing up'). The topmost leaves remain visible. Repeat two more
times during the season resulting in ridges.

2. Pile leaves, grass cuttings, compost etc. around the plants when available.
This is to exclude light and stop the new potatoes turning green.

Watering is most important when the potatoes are starting to form.

Fertility: High requirement.

Harvest: Harvesting of the earliest varieties can begin at the end of June.

1. Carefully dig along the line of the trench (not from the side to avoid spearing
the tubers).

2. Part the grass and organic matter from the base of the stems and pull up the
plants. Most tubers should be attached or on the soil surface. Leave to dry before
putting in thick paper sacks.

Origins and Varieties

Potatoes have been grown in South America, particularly Peru, for over 7000
years. They were brought over to the UK and Ireland by Sir John Hawkins, Sir
Francis Drake and Sir Walter Raleigh – in that order. It appears that you get a
knighthood for supplying potatoes.

In the 19th century, breeding was carried using selections of Chilean potatoes that
didn't need the increasingly shorter days to promote tuber formation, as with

most of our (maincrop) potatoes. What we got were the first First and Second earlies which produce a crop earlier in the year.

The disease, potato blight, was apparently first brought to Europe when a holdfull of rotting potatoes was dumped on the quayside in Dublin by a ship from North America. This spread rapidly through Irish crops over the next few years, mainly because only one (susceptible) variety was being grown. It's strange to think, what with the enormous popularity of potatoes in our time, that when they were first brought to Europe, they were regarded in France with suspicion and disgust, as poisonous tubers. The King had to eat potatoes in public to persuade the population to overcome their aversion. In Scotland, people were persuaded to avoid potatoes because they weren't mentioned in the Bible.

First-early varieties tend to avoid blight because they are out of the ground before it gets going, usually in the summer. Maincrop (or Late) spuds are still growing, or trying to, in August. Established, reliable varieties include 'Maris Bard', 'Pentland Javelin' and 'Arran Pilot'. 'Accent' continues to grow if not harvested early.

Second-early varieties (started and harvested a little later than Firsts) include 'Kestrel', 'Charlotte', 'Vivaldi' and 'Cosmos'.

Pests and Diseases
Late blight, slugs, potato cyst eelworm and other assorted hole-making insects and rots.

Comments
Early potatoes are grown because they are harvested, well, early. They're also usually planted before any others, making another reason to call them early. Another common difference between Earlies and Maincrop (though not a water-tight one) is waxiness. Many earlies are waxy, salad potatoes, good for boiling.

'Seed' potatoes are theoretically virus-free spuds from a garden centre/seed merchant and are about the size of a small hen's egg. Larger than this means you can use slightly wider spacings. The practice of cutting up large tubers is a last resort: they have the potential to rot so leave the cut surfaces to dry before planting. Also, each half has to have some 'eyes' (little buds found towards one end – called the rose end) meaning that the cut has to be lengthways.

For this group (earlies), chitting is a valuable process. Set the seed potatoes with most of the eyes/buds facing upwards in a cool, light, frost-free place as soon as you get them (This is a better use of egg boxes even than for eggs).

Ideally keep them like that for several weeks, even months, meaning buy them early e.g. January. Stubby green shoots should appear and this will give the plants a head start when they go out in March. In other words, your early potatoes just got earlier.

Trying to find a cool, frost-free, light location is not easy. Perhaps turn off the heating in the kids' bedroom and explain to them that it's a choice between eating or pulling on another jumper.

Chitting doesn't help the later types much, though seeing as you've got to do something with the tubers between buying and planting – why not chit them? Earlies are not the heaviest yielding (get maincrops if you want that): they're dug up before they have finished growing.

It is possible to grow earlies with a very late planting, so that you get new potatoes for Christmas, Solstice, or whatever. But is it worth the effort? They have to be pampered – kept out of frost, etc. – and it isn't as if there aren't any potatoes around then: lovely, fluffy, stored maincrop, ready for roasting and baking.

On the previous page you are given two alternatives in how to grow spuds: one is the traditional trench method, but number two is a fascinating way of getting a good yield without digging. The seed potato is on the surface and the new potatoes form around it. Harvesting is dead easy: the organic matter is parted and the potatoes lifted out. A little careful tweaking with a trowel might help uncover any shy tubers in the area.

There has to be a catch or two: you need lots of leaves, grass, etc.: in a dry summer this may be an issue. Also, if for some reason a hole appears in this layer, you'll get green potatoes that are hard to cook and make you feel unwell when eaten.

It's still worth trying. The soil is wonderful for the crops that follow, too.

Potatoes, Maincrop

Naming – as for early potatoes

A NEGLECTED
SEED POTATO

Planting

When: Mid-April

Where: Prepared bed outside, possibly containers.

How: As for Earlies, with a spacing of 75cm (2ft 6ins) between rows and 38cm (15ins) between potatoes. This spacing is for seed potatoes of small egg (hens) size. Larger seed means wider spacing; smaller means closer.

Using 1.2m (4ft) beds, the row spacing is too wide for the traditional digging method which requires earthing up: try 60cm (2ft) rows with 45cm (18ins) between potatoes.

Fertility: High requirement; most applied as organic matter at planting.

Harvest: Lift as required, but for maximum yield wait until the tops have died down in the early autumn. If the leaves are diseased with blight, remove the tops and wait a couple of weeks before lifting. Let the lifted potatoes dry before putting in a paper or hessian sack. Any rejects can be used straight away or, if beyond consumption, stamped on and composted. Keep the sack in a dark, cool, frost-free, dry, mouse-proof place.

Varieties

There is a huge range of varieties to choose from, with different purposes. Firstly, there are slightly earlier and later maincrops. Secondly, there is their use, and you can find varieties specifically for mashing, boiling, chips, etc. Personally, I haven't the room to grow many different varieties so trust that the one I go for covers a range of uses. Generally, maincrops are floury/fluffy with the occasional waxy variety (usually only for boiling): it's worth distinguishing between the two. An older variety like 'Desiree', recommended particularly as a baked potato, will do very well roasted or mashed.

'Pink Fir Apple' is a waxy, salad maincrop and well worth growing for its flavour, if not yield. When you look at the price they command in the shops (if you can find them) that's even more of an incentive to grow them.

Colour is another factor to consider with more than just red or white now being available. 'Edzell Blue' has both blue skin and flesh, 'Setanta', a recent introduction, has red skin and yellow flesh.

Perhaps high on the list should be pest and disease resistance. 'Sárpo Mira' and 'Sárpo Axona' are amongst the best for resistance against blight. There is a small question mark against the flavour of some of the Sárpo varieties: perhaps try them for yourself and don't leave them in the ground too long – they become starchier as the season progresses. Some varieties, it is claimed, are resistant to slugs, e.g. 'Romano'.

Comments

What is it about potatoes that summarises vegetable growing as the true delight that it is. The interring of a 'seed' and covering its face, nurturing it and then the harvest – the thrill of discovery as these little nuggets seem to appear from nowhere.

Anyway, if you're short of space, I wouldn't bother. I reckon they take up a lot of ground, water and nutrients to grow and organic potatoes are relatively cheap to buy. Save your land for more unusual, expensive or hard-to-find crops. There is definitely an argument for trying early potatoes; or something a bit weird, like purple maincrops or the tasty 'Pink Fir Apple'.

Let us indulge in a little botany. Potatoes aren't root vegetables. The tuber is – wait for it – the swollen end of an underground stem (rhizome). For that reason, it is believed that 'earthing up' (see earlies) encourages more rhizomes and hence more potatoes. In practice there is not a huge increase. Even the method of gradually stacking up tyres and filling them with compost as the plant grows still only results in spuds in the bottom tyre.

It is often said that potatoes are a 'cleaning' crop and the foliage can be dense enough to suppress weeds. However, it is the way they are grown that has most effect: either earthing up or thick mulches prevent weed growth. Despite all of this, don't plant potatoes into ex-grassland to get it cleared – the resulting crop will be full of holes from wireworm and leatherjackets that were happily living in lawns or old meadows and still want something to eat. Maincrop potatoes are most affected by late blight, because they are, well, late. They crop more heavily than earlies, but are slower to bulk up and are harvested usually when the tops die down. Blight often attacks in July and, particularly August, after earlies.

The organic defence of cutting off all the tops as soon as the leaves are attacked by blight, saves the tubers from being affected but stops the crops in their tracks. Ideally, we need resistant varieties, but Mr. Blight is a tricky sort of chap and changes (or mutates) when you're not looking. In its latest incarnation, dubbed the catchy A2 Blue 13, the dreaded blight overcame the resistance of many of the old varieties. But help is at hand thanks to the delightful Hungarians with their incomprehensible language: 'Sárpo' varieties have saved the day (until the next blight mutation, that is). In a mild autumn, 'Sárpos' are still in full leaf in October. Forget G.M. potatoes – 'Sárpo' types should be our breeding stock. Pronounced 'sharpo' by the way (approximately).

Another affliction to trouble our spuds is one most people don't know about. The potato cyst eelworm (or nematode) is a tiny worm which feeds on the roots in such numbers as to, at best, reduce yields and at worst, stop plants completely. If you've ever wondered why a particular plant is stunted or has collapsed, well, it might be this (though it could also be slugs and a dozen other things). The eggs reside in the soil and hatch when a potato grows nearby; the essence of potato leaking out stimulates them to do so. Bad news: the little stinkers can survive in the soil for 20 years, though they do decline over that time. So, as long a rotation as possible can help a certain amount, as can the growing of a related plant called *Solanum sisymbriifolium*. This unpronounceable plant, if sown prior to your potato crop, stimulates the eggs to hatch and the resulting eelworms die when they find no potatoes to infest, possibly from disappointment. Result? When you pop in your seed potatoes – a cleaned up soil.

As with earlies, tubers exposed to light will have a green tinge to them. If you think about it, this is a fairly sensible thing to do: a bit of stem given enough light might as well start photosynthesising. This not only makes them difficult to cook (they stay hard) but they aren't terribly good for you. The green-ness is simply chlorophyll but it is accompanied by a defence mechanism (if the tuber is near the surface then it is more vulnerable): a mild toxin of the same ilk as cocaine, nicotine and strychnine. It is a steroid alkaloid, if you really wanted to know, which will make you feel a bit queasy if you eat too many. Pregnant women should avoid them completely apparently.

The timing of watering is important with potatoes: a little to establish, then ease off until the tubers are 'marble size' when we should ladle it on. How do we know they are marble size? We can peek, with the same thrill and guilt (almost) of peeping through a keyhole; or, we can guess: about June?

We can make a calculated gamble on it being at the same time as flowering (which is different for different varieties).

Alternatively, we can just not worry about it, and do it when we remember.

Radish

Raphanus sativa
(*Raphanus*, possibly from Greek *ra phaino* – quickly, I grow; s*ativa*, cultivated)
Family: BRASSICACEAE

Sowing

When: Repeated sowings from March onwards, every two weeks. They can be sown earlier with protection. Winter and oriental varieties are sown July/August.

Where: Direct sowing in a prepared bed (rotation with cabbages).

How: Seed drills 1.5cm (¾in) deep and 15cm (6ins) apart. Thin seedlings to 2.5cm (1in) apart.

Fertility: Medium requirement, but often considered high, when included with other brassicas.

Harvest: After around 4 weeks, selectively and carefully pull up plants when you can see the top of the swollen root.

'SCARLET GLOBE' AND MILD FLEA BEETLE DAMAGE

Origin and Varieties

So many of our common vegetables seem to come from the eastern Mediterranean and western Asia. Well, there was a lot going on there a few millennia ago – trade routes, successive major empires – so perhaps it's not surprising that a bit of energy got put into horticulture. The Egyptians, Greeks, Romans, etc. all enjoyed a nice radish.

For a typical round, red object, the summer varieties 'Scarlet Globe' (the name says it all) and 'Cherry Belle' seem to have been around forever, as has the slightly elongated, white-tipped 'French Breakfast'. There are other colours, like the self-explanatory 'Icicle' and the winter 'Round Spanish Black'. Also of interest is mooli or daikon, a Japanese monster radish that looks like a giant white carrot and is great in stir fry, or grated in salads. The different varieties of this oriental specimen are juicy, mild in flavour and best left in the ground until required.

Pests and Diseases

Flea beetle, other brassica P & D if the radishes are in the ground for a long time.

Comments

If you were exceptionally hungry, you could say 'I'm absolutely *Raphanus*.' But then you might not.

Radishes aren't perhaps the best choice to satisfy hunger, mainly because of the mustard oils that make them 'hot'. The hotness is dependent on the variety, to a certain degree, but mainly on you: if you leave them too long they become fiery little golf balls. The task, therefore, is to ensure a steady supply of young roots. Sowing short rows every couple of weeks is the target but is rarely achieved for one of the following reasons:

We make the rows too long and feel bad about throwing away the excess and sowing a new lot.

We lose the plot – 'was that fourth sowing last week or the week before or where is it?'

We don't like radishes.

Records would be a help: a note of what is being sown when and where (see 'Rotations'); but a more relaxed approach could be broadcast sowing. Scatter a few seeds thinly in a patch between young cabbage plants, for example, then work them into the soil surface using the points of a fork or by gently bouncing the tines of a rake over the area. You can simply do this when it occurs to you – a recipe for chaos for some of us, but might just do the trick for others. However, it is still important to thin out the seedlings.

Success with radishes is achieved by the fact that they are in and out of the ground in a very short space of time. Being part of the brassica family, they are subject to a wide range of pests and diseases, but most of these don't get a chance to take hold before the roots are consumed. The exception is flea beetle, a tiny, shiny black, sometimes striped, creature that is ready and waiting to make lots of little holes in the leaves as soon as the seedling emerges. A sheet of fleece is exceptionally useful for protecting germinating radishes.

As with other root vegetables, watering should be moderate and steady; too much and you get lots of leaf with, if anything, a miniature red bead at the bottom. Too little and they will be hotter, tougher and more likely to go to seed. There is a variety called 'Sangria' which is specially for the leaves, not the root: cut and use as for rocket and other loose salad leaves.

For the real adventurer there is the vaguely exciting idea of sowing radishes to eat their fruit instead. With one sowing of a variety like 'Serpent' or 'Munchen Bier', the large top growth produces masses of 5-7.5cm (2-3ins) green pods. These are crisp, of a mild peppery flavour, and ideal for stir fries. They must, however, be picked regularly and whilst young, and after a while this becomes a bit of a hassle, as a result of which the whole plant gets abandoned. But there again, that might just be me.

Rocket

Eruca sativa

(*Eruca,* Latin name for a related plant; *sativa,* cultivated)

Family: BRASSICACEAE

Sowing

When: March to August

Where: Modules/cells or direct in the ground (rotation with cabbages).

How: About three seeds in each cell; no need to thin. If direct, sow thinly in rows 15cm (6ins) apart, thin to 15cm (6ins) intervals, or leave and cut as required.

Transplanting

When: When two true leaves are on each plant – about 5cm (2ins) high.

Where: Prepared bed outside, possibly intercropped amongst other plants like other slow-growing brassicas.

'ROQUETTE' - A POSH BIT OF ROCKET

Rocket works very well in containers.

How: Space transplants about 15cm (6ins) apart in each direction.

Fertility: Medium requirement, despite being a brassica.

Harvest: Clear cut plants about 2.5cm (1in) above the soil for them to regrow, or selectively remove the older leaves as required.

Origin and Varieties

A Mediterranean plant, rocket was harvested wild across the entire region from Turkey to Portugal. Cultivation is recorded with the Romans. It is only in recent years that it has been grown in this country in any quantity.

Salad rocket is an annual and shouldn't be confused in your rotation with wild rocket, *Diplotaxis tenuifolia,* which is a perennial (permanent) plant. See 'Comments' for other similar salads.

Pests and Diseases

Flea beetle, slugs

Comments

With a name as straightforward and, let's face it, exciting as 'rocket', it is a bit baffling to find that in the USA it is called 'arugula', which is like the sound someone makes whilst gargling soup.

Is rocket the epitome of trendy vegetables? It only seriously appeared on the UK scene 30 odd years ago, and then as a fancy garnish to accompany a drizzle of something exotic on a plate, looking like someone forgot to do the washing up.

No self-respecting salad bag would be sold nowadays without a good helping of rocket in it. Other ingredients may include leafy vegetables grown in a very similar way and at the same time of year as rocket. They include mizuna, mibuna and various kinds of mustard leaf. Also in our bag could be seedling crops such as kale, or a whole range of little plants like corn salad (lamb's lettuce) and claytonia (miner's lettuce), depending on the time of year; not to mention, of course, lettuce.

Let us pin down a few common features of rocket, mizuna, mibuna and mustards:

1. They get hotter in flavour the older they are.

They are semi-hardy, meaning you will get leaves over winter if they are protected.

2. They don't last long before flowering at hot times of year. Provide shade and moisture if possible to avoid stressing the plants in the summer.

3. You can pick individual leaves or clear cut and hope for some re-growth (cut-and-come-again).

4. You can sow thinly in rows or in clumps directly in the ground, or in modules.

5. They do particularly well in the second half of the year, with the length of day getting shorter; this is actually essential if you want to grow Pak Choi and the like.

6. They are all brassicas, so can be fitted (intercropped) amongst other slower-growing brassicas.

Quick-growing plants make some things so much easier. For instance, there is less of a demand on the soil. This makes them very suitable for containers: the pests and diseases don't have so much of a chance to get a hold, whereas other long-term brassicas are well afflicted. Even flea beetle, which loves hot dry conditions, won't be around so much at the best time of year to grow rocket, i.e. autumn into winter. Slugs would far prefer a fat lettuce to speedy rocket.

A couple of alternatives to some of the above: the variety 'Esmee', being slow to bolt, is supposed to be a good choice for summer sowing. And wild rocket, which is a perennial and therefore should provide us with leaves in the hungry gap, might not be quite so good as anticipated: the seed catalogues recommend us to sow it afresh each year for the best texture and flavour. But then they might just be trying to sell us more seeds.....

Vitamin levels are good in rocket, including C, all of which, is available, because it is eaten raw and not cooked – chew well. On top of all of that, according to my buds, the taste is great.

With rocket we have gastronomical lift off.

Spinach

Spinacia oleracea
(*Spinacia*, from the Latin *spina*, a prickle; *oleracea*, of the garden)
Family: AMARANTHACEAE

Sowing

When: Anytime of year, preferably autumn or early
spring (March/April).

Where: Sow directly in the ground (rotation with
beetroot).

How: In rows 30cm (12ins) apart, seeds about 2.5cm
(1in) apart. Thin plants to 20-25cm (810ins) spacing.
Use the thinnings in salads etc.

Fertility: Medium requirement.

Harvest: For fresh young leaves remove the whole
plant (see 'Comments'), selectively remove the older
leaves or clear cut the whole plant above the growing
point, to allow re-growth.

AN ARROWHEAD OR
GOOSE'S ROOT OF
SPINACH

Origin and Varieties

Spinach is a relative latecomer to the UK, not mentioned as being in cultivation
here before the 16th century.

Originally from the Middle East, it wandered off to China before eventually
making it to Europe via north Africa. In Italy, Spain, France and other lands they
have similar, 'spinachy' names for it which may have given rise to the Latin
name, *Spinacia,* or alternatively, they could have got it from the Latin *spina*
meaning prickly (the seeds had spiky coats).

You can now get varieties with prickly or smooth spinach seed, the former
varieties tend to be hardier, but the latter are said to be less likely to go to seed
prematurely in a hot summer.

It's always a wise move to get a variety with multiple properties. A hardy,
prickly-seeded type for autumn sowing is 'Giant Winter', which also has good
disease-resistance; plus, it can be sown as a summer crop. Similarly,
'Medania', though a round-seeded type, can be sown at any time of year and
has good mildew resistance.

Pests and Diseases

Slugs, aphids, downy mildew

Comments

Spinach has perhaps had the greatest publicity of any vegetable. Children
notoriously dislike green vegetables – possibly just to annoy their parents – but
apparently, they also have over three times the number of taste buds that adults

do. As a result, they can detect bitterness and other unpleasant flavours more easily or acutely. Maybe that's an evolutionary trick to stop the little blighters eating all and sundry when they're wandering around the countryside etc.

Anyway, they overcame this prejudice purely because Popeye, the cartoon sailor man, told them to, flexing his bulging biceps as proof of its efficacy.

Us older blighters are tempted to say: 'Well done, Popeye'. There are plenty of minerals like iron and vitamins A and C, plus enough antioxidants to give a leg up to any cell in need of support. However, there are one or two small issues to deal with:

Firstly, the levels of nutrients aren't quite as stupendous as was initially thought, particularly for iron, because the 19th century doctor testing spinach got the decimal point in the wrong place.

Secondly, spinach is in the same family as beetroot and chard, which can have an excess of a substance called oxalic acid. This stuff gives rhubarb its teeth-furring properties. Oxalic acid can bind to the iron and calcium in spinach leaves, thereby stopping the body from absorbing them. It might be worth considering the oxalic acid factor if you have joint or bone issues, such as arthritis.

Fortunately, there are lower levels of oxalic acid found in young plants and young parts of older plants.

Therefore, our aim should perhaps be to harvest spinach once only per sowing (a 'destructive harvest'), as opposed to cutting and allowing regrowth or gradually picking, as recommended for lettuce.

To support this, spinach can bolt very quickly, especially in hot weather, so it doesn't last long anyway. Grow it early in the year, or even over-winter it with a bit of protection.

If you want to have spinach during the summer, then here are a few suggestions to help you do so:

- Grow it in a shady place; perhaps break the rotation (just a bit) by having a row or two down the middle of your runner beans.
- Use bolt-resistant varieties.
- Ensure that the plants have plenty of moisture, i.e. organic matter in the soil and adequate watering.
- Grow chard/perpetual spinach instead.

A couple of interesting facts to finish with.

Spinach is used as a green pigment for food dyeing. How about dyeing some mashed potato green to make it more exciting and to sneak spinach into your kid's meals?

Like many of our vegetables, the nutrient content declines after harvest (by about a half within a week) so freeze straight away if you can't use it there and then. Of course, growing your own and cutting as required might be best of all.....

Squash (winter) and Pumpkins

Cucurbita pepo, C. maxma, C. moschata
(*Cucurbita*, Latin for gourd; *pepo*, from Greek, *pepon*, edible gourd,
maxima, largest, *moschata*, musky) Family: CUCURBITACEAE

Sowing
When: April/May
Where: Pots or large modules/cells.
How: Push the seeds on their edge into the
compost, one per pot. This gets them deep into the
pot and, apparently, stops them rotting compared to
lying flat. Aim for 20°C to germinate.

Transplanting
When: End of May/after the last frost *Where:*
Prepared bed outside.

A BADLY-CUT HUBBARD
BLUE SQUASH

How: Plant with compost added to the hole; don't
disturb the roots. Spacing depends on type of
squash and the catalogue/book. Go for approx. 1m (3ft) each direction; it's
easier to remember. There may be a bit of space between bush types and the
trailing types may intermingle.

Fertility: High requirement – mulch after planting with compost. *Harvest:*
Remove fruit before heavy frosts. Leave stalk intact and carry the fruit as
though it is a bowl of soup. Leave to 'cure' (i.e. let the skin toughen) in the sun
for 7-10 days. Protect from frost. Store at 7-15°C, with medium humidity, yet
good air circulation and they should keep for months, depending on variety.
Is this the time the unheated spare bedroom comes into its own? It's a good
excuse to stop relatives staying.

Origins and Varieties
Squash and pumpkins are from the Americas, where the original wild forms
were collected for their seeds. They have been in cultivation for around 10
millenia and made it to Europe following the colonisation of America in the 16th
Century.

The sizes and shapes of squash range from the rather beautiful to the deeply
worrying, with names following a similar pattern: 'Delicata' to 'Uchiki Kuri'
(pronounced as 'you cheeky curry'); 'Sweet Dumpling' to 'Twonga'.
For small pumpkins, try 'Baby Bear' or 'Jack Be Little', for hopefully big ones
there's 'Atlantic Giant'.

Pests and Diseases
Slugs and snails, powdery mildew, aphids, cucumber mosaic virus.

Comments

A vegetable (though, of course, technically a fruit) that wasn't much in evidence in this country a generation ago. A splendid import from the States, pumpkins haven't gained quite the popularity here as they have over the pond, whereas the range and versatility of squash have really taken off. The word squash comes from the Native American word 'askutasquash' meaning something like 'a green thing eaten raw', which doesn't help much.

These plants, as opposed to courgettes, marrows and summer squash, are storable, provided they have been 'cured' (meaning the skins have been toughened up by exposing to higher temperatures, often after harvesting). How well they keep depends on the variety.

As often, with non-native plants, a little extra care has to be taken to get anything half decent at the end, and with squash the emphasis is on warmth, moisture and nutrients. 'Aha', you say, 'But that is the same for all vegetables'. Well, stop interrupting: I was going to say that it requires these three in greater quantities. Adequate food and water is largely up to us and, as usual, can be aided by the addition of organic matter. The tricky bit is warmth. We can use cloches or polytunnels and these will do the trick, except this book is particularly about outdoor vegetables, plus some of these plants can get quite large (see below). As long as there are relatively high temperatures at some point in the summer, you should get a crop. There have been times when the squash plants have been put out and have just sat there for a month or two, going a bit yellow and looking as miserable as a holidaymaker on the beach at around the same time. Then the temperature flies up to the dizzy heights of the upper 20's – the starting pistol has gone – and the squash are off. For some varieties, like butternut, the temperature needs to be sustained for several months, and for that reason these are some of the more difficult to succeed with.

These vegetables must have plenty of room. Some are described as having a 'bush habit' and rather than referring to a curious substance abuse, this means it will grow and stay in the same place, producing a mound of foliage. Most have a 'trailing habit', meaning the stems will reach across the soil surface like octopus tentacles and, inevitably, go in completely the opposite direction to that you desired. Some, like the wonderful 'Sweet Dumpling', are semi-trailing, meaning it can't make up its mind.

You can try training long stems over things like trellis or bending them round or even cutting the ends off. I quite like them rummaging through neighbouring crops, which can usually cope, it being near the end of the season when this happens.

Good news is that they are fairly pest- and disease-free except, of course, for the obligatory slugs and snails, which go for the young plants and the flowers and

77

fruit as they form. Occasionally, they succumb to powdery mildew, but if you keep the plants well fed and watered this is less likely.

There is much variation within the squashes including the growth habit, the yield (typically, the larger the fruit the fewer you will get), colour, texture including moist/dry and smooth/fibrous, storability and, of course, flavour. Let us do a little generalising: many *C. pepo* have smooth flesh which is quite sweet e.g. 'Delicata' and the pumpkins. Many *C. maxima* have drier, nutty flesh making them excellent for roasting e.g. 'Green Hokkaido' and 'Black Futsu' and *C. moschata*, typified by the giant-peanut, buff-coloured butternut, is great for soup but less exciting in other ways. It would be really helpful if it was as straightforward as that because then you could decide on the squash you'd like (when buying) by looking at the stalks: *C. pepo* has a hard, angled stalk (it would look a bit like a star in cross section) while *C. maxima* has a squat, knobbly, corky thing. And you know what a butternut squash looks like (its stalk is hard and a bit angled, if you were interested). Whilst on the subject of being rude about squashes, I'm not a major fan of pumpkins. Yes, you can lose them in a stew/soup but the only reason why a pumpkin pie is a success seems to be the sugar and cream. Of course, you can grow them to decorate / carve / smash / compost if you're less interested in feeding yourself. There is a possible exception: 'Lady Godiva' is an amusingly-named hybrid pumpkin with lots of shell-less (naked) seeds inside, easy to eat without fiddling around trying to get the seedcoat off.

One more variety to finish with. 'Marina di Chioggia' is a medium to large *C. maxima* squash which can store until the following May, with the flavour getting better with time. Worth contemplating.

Swedes

Brassica napus Napobrassica group
(*Brassica*, Latin for cabbage; *napus*, Latin for turnip;
Napobrassica, turnip-cabbage) Family:
BRASSICACEAE

Sowing

When: One sowing in April/May/June (unlike
turnips that are sown in succession).
Where: Direct in a prepared seedbed. (rotation with
cabbages).
How: Sow in drills 45cm (18ins) apart – on a 1.2m
(4ft) bed this means three rows.
Sow thinly then thin out to about 15cm (6ins) apart.
Alternatively, sow two or three seeds at a spacing of
30cm (12ins) in all directions, thinning to one
seedling.
Fertility: Medium requirement, but the rest of this
family needs high fertility.
Harvest: Swedes are ready to use after 4.5-6 months
growing. They can be left in the ground with some

CABBAGE ROOT FLY
LARVA AND HOME

protection or lifted and stored like carrots in a humid and cool environment.
Twist the leaves off and pack in damp sand in a cool, frost-free place.

Origins and Varieties

Swedes came from... Sweden, where, as a cross between turnip and cabbage, it
was growing wild. It was a late introduction to this country, in the 18th century. It
is called rutabaga in North America, after the Swedish name.
The main use of turnips and swedes was as animal fodder; a convenient winter
storage food.
Only a handful of varieties are readily available. 'Marian' and 'Ruby' are
reliable, tasty and with good disease resistance.

Pests and Diseases

Mildew, clubroot, cabbage root fly, flea beetle

Comments

It's nice when things match up, so here's a little morsel: the word swede is short
for Swedish turnip and the 'nip' bit of turnip has the same origin as the
Scottish 'neep' (as in neeps and tatties) and the Latin 'napus', meaning turnip.
The 'turn' part means 'make round', presumably as in wood turning. Well, that's
the interesting part out of the way.

Reasons to grow swedes? They're tastier than turnips (that's official): sweet, golden mounds of steaming mashed neeps. Wonderful, unless you're in the half of the population that can't stand them.

Key points to follow with swedes are: thin early and keep uniformly moist throughout the growing season. A good mulch of compost when the plants are up and running will, as ever, help enormously.

They're grown in the same way as turnips, sowing directly in beautifully straight rows, though swedes need a lot more space since they have bigger roots. Other major differences are that swedes take a lot longer to mature but are hardier, so can be left *in situ* through winter to harvest as required (the less attractive maincrop turnips can also be stored this way). Some can even be left until the spring when the leafy re-growth can be used like spinach. Be aware that swedes can become coarse and woody if left in the ground all winter.

Harvesting size should be anything from golf ball to cricket ball (though not so hard), or if you prefer a change of sport, squash ball to tennis ball (though not so soft). With the wide spacing (previous page) you should get the larger version, at least. In a row of swedes, you can selectively pull the size you want.

At Halloween, big swedes were the carved lantern of choice for many years in the UK. This was before the huge grinning pumpkins appeared from the States. Dredging the distant memory of this time, another feature, apart from the gentle odour of burning swede, was the fact that you carried your lantern. Perhaps this was tradition or maybe it was because the bottoms of swedes aren't flat like pumpkins, so you can't set them down easily.

Anyway, it's all probably a lot safer now; you haven't got irresponsible juveniles swinging lighted vegetables around the place, just scary pumpkins setting fire to the curtains instead.

Brassicas are prone to a wide range of pests and diseases, and swedes and turnips are no exception, though some have less of an effect, like cabbage white butterfly.

Sweet Corn

Zea mays

(*Zea*, from the Greek for another cereal; *mays*, from the Mexican name for maize)

Family: POACEAE

Sowing

When: April

Where: In deep modules (cells) or pots. *How:*
Fill the modules with compost, firm, make a hole
with a pencil about 3cm (1in) deep and drop in one
seed. Cover over and keep in a warm place (about
20°C).

Transplanting

When: End of May

Where: In open ground in a prepared bed. They
can have a block of the rotation to themselves.

How: Space plants 30-45cm (12-18ins) apart in a
block.

RIPENING COB AND
SWEET-TOOTHED VISITOR

Fertility: High requirement.

Harvest: Break off the cob when the tassels emerging from the end have gone
brown, or, more accurately, when the liquid in the kernels has changed from
being watery to milky but before it has become thick (doughy). Most varieties
start to deteriorate as soon as they have been harvested, the sugars turning
rapidly to starches. A connoisseur might have a pan of water boiling on the
allotment camping stove before harvesting. There has recently been a move to
breeding new varieties with longer-lasting cobs.

Origins and Varieties

Sweet corn originates from the bowels of the Americas and was introduced to
Europe in the 16th century. Because of the relatively shorter, cooler summers in
the UK, it didn't really get going until we had new quicker maturing varieties…
and global warming.

F1 hybrids are the big success story for sweet corn. Nothing like the heinous
genetically-manipulated plants, they are still highly bred. Still, the results for
sweet corn mean we can have a crop more reliably produced than old open-
pollinated types. Breeding has also focussed on sweetness. This is lovely to a
certain degree and is less of an issue than with, say, apples, where we are
inundated with execrable varieties like Gala, which are bred for sweetness and
being crisp and juicy, ignoring all of the subtle aromatic flavours in older
varieties.

81

If you want to grow sweet corn on an allotment, then avoid a group called 'super sweets': they need to be over eight metres from other varieties otherwise the cobs will have been cross pollinated and turn them into 'sadly unsweets'. Your neighbours will almost certainly have sweet corn.

Pests and Diseases

Badgers, frit fly, birds, mice.

Comments

The names given to sweet corn are a bit confusing (hence the unambiguous use of Latin names). There is 'corn', often used to refer to any cereal, such as wheat. There is 'maize', a word particularly related to processed sweet corn and animal food, and there is 'corn-on-the-cob' – cooked sweet corn. There is an image I have of eating a cob of sweet corn row by row, from side to side, like the movement of the carriage of an old-fashioned typewriter. There just needs to be a little 'ting' at the end of each row. Those of you brought up on computer keyboards will wonder what this is all about, so let us get on to something more straightforward about sweet corn:

They are monoecious, wind-pollinated monocotyledons. It is good to have made that clear.

Actually, this is useful information. Here's why: monoecious means there are separate male and female flowers on the same plant, the male is the feathery plume right at the top and the female flower has tassels (thin strands) emerging, and is near the bottom of the plant.

Wind pollination means that if you want to get any cobs, the pollen has to move from the male flowers to the females on other plants.

This all tells us that if we plant sweet corn in a long thin row, the pollen will drift and 'miss'. We should set them out in a grid pattern, ideally a square. Poor pollination shows as a cob with kernels absent, especially near the tip. Seed can be sown directly into the ground (especially useful if you forgot to do the indoor sowing). However, you must ensure the soil has warmed up sufficiently. This can be done artificially with plastic or by waiting until, usually, the end of May/beginning of June. If this is done, use a relatively fast-maturing type: the quickest is about 90 days from sowing.

Watering is required to establish plants; then restrain yourself. However, when the plant starts flowering and fruiting, a lot of its energy is diverted away from the root system. This means that sweet corn is very responsive to watering at this time.

Time to step up onto the soapbox: vast swathes of sweet corn/maize (or any cereal for that matter) are not good news. Firstly, most of it is used to feed intensively-reared animals, which is an extraordinarily inefficient use of our land. Plus, as mentioned, they are wind-pollinated. Couple this with high herbicide use and you have a landscape completely devoid of insect pollinated flowers. No wild flowers, no insects, no birds.

What a crazy world.

Tomatoes

Solanum lycopersicum

(*Solanum,,*classical Latin for the nightshades; *lycopersicum*, from Greek
meaning wolf-peach) Family: SOLANACEAE

Sowing

When: April

Where: Indoors in pots or modules (cells).

How: Keep warm to germinate (~20°C). Two seeds
per sowing, thin to the strongest plant.

Transplanting

When: End of May or after the last frost, whenever
that is.

Where: Outside in prepared beds (rotation with
potatoes). Outside in containers or borders (cordon
types). For bush types see 'Comments'.

HAPPY
END-OF-SEASON
TOMATOES

How: Space bush types at 45cm (18ins) giving a
double, staggered row on a 1.2m (4ft) bed. This close spacing gives the highest
yield per sq.m, plus makes fruiting earlier. Cordon types: minimum size of
container 25cm (10ins).

Fertility: High requirement, particularly potassium (see 'Fertility').

Harvest: When the fruit are fully ripe the sides of the fruit have some 'give';
unripe fruit, ripening off the plant (as per supermarket fruit), never tastes as
good. Overripe fruit can split, as it does towards the end of the season anyway.

Origins and Varieties

Tomatoes were brought to Europe in the 16th century but took quite a while to
get going. They require warm conditions, so were not grown widely in northern
Europe until more recent times.

They seem to have had good and bad press along the way. Often thought to be
poisonous (they are a member of the Deadly Nightshade family) they were then
considered to be an aphrodisiac (a 'love apple'). Nowadays, they are praised for
their vitamins and antioxidants, especially lycopene that is an aid to preventing
heart disease.

There are hundreds of tomato varieties, many wonderful shapes, sizes, colours
and flavours.

For bush tomatoes, the range is more limited: 'Red Alert' – small, red, 'San
Marzano' – plum, red, 'Golden Nugget' – small, yellow, early, 'Koralik' – red
cherry, reasonable blight resistance.

For cordons: 'Ailsa Craig' – traditional red; 'Gardener's Delight' – small, red, less vigorous; 'Tigerella' – medium, red-yellow stripes. 'Crimson Crush' – medium-large red, very blight-resistant, suitable for outdoors. And many more.

Pests and Diseases (outside)

Blight, aphids, blossom end rot, verticillium wilt.

Comments

Wolf-peach, eh? The Greeks weren't really indicating that this is a 'vicious stone-fruit' – it means more like 'inferior peach'. I suppose if you were eating a tomato expecting a peach, it would be.

Since we are concerned with growing vegetables outside, the tomatoes to look at are, not surprisingly, outdoor types, plus some indoor types that we can get away with outdoors.

The outdoor types first: they have a bushy habit and need little attention apart from feeding and watering. If possible, help them to keep warm with a cloche. If they aren't given this, one year out of two you won't get a single ripe tomato: either the plant succumbs to disease (the same blight that affects potatoes) or the summer isn't good enough to ripen the clusters of green fruit hunched together, shivering.

The indoor types have been developed for greenhouses and they are grown on a single stem (a cordon) trained up a string or cane. We can get away with growing them outside if they are in a sheltered place – against a shed, wall, etc. Because of that they are often cultivated in pots or grow-bags.

To make a tomato stay at just one stem, it requires 'side-shooting' – removal of the little shoots that appear at the junction of a leaf and the main stem. This also keeps the plant concentrated on fruit production. Use your thumb and forefinger to snap them off. You have to be vigilant: completely side-shooting the toms before going away for the weekend feels good, except when you come back there are always one or two shoots the length of an arm, cheerily waving to you. Worry not. Take them off as soon as you see them. Cordons are usually 'stopped' at five clusters of flowers or fruit: the stem is cut off just above the fifth one. This is trying to be realistic about what is achievable in a normal summer. Given more protection, or great weather, they can be left to go on a lot longer.

Feeding is more important with tomatoes than most vegetables, especially if they are in containers. Comfrey liquid is ideal and there are also specially formulated organic tomato feeds, often made from seaweed. Using urine works very well, diluted 1:20 at each watering: tomatoes seem to cope well with the salt content. However, there is nothing more likely to put you off your salad than someone gaily announcing that 'the tomatoes are made from my wee'.

Turnips

Brassica rapa Rapifera Group
(*Brassica*, Latin for the cabbage tribe; *rapa*, of rape;
Rapifera – plants that are like rape)
Family: BRASSICACEAE

Sowing

When: Earlies: March onwards. Maincrop: June
Where: Direct into a prepared seed bed (rotation
with cabbages). Could be grown in containers.
How: Earlies are sown closely (about 22cm (9ins)
between rows) and thinned to 10cm (4ins) apart.
Maincrop varieties are in rows 30cm (12ins) apart
and are thinned to 15cm (6ins).
Fertility: Medium requirement, but included with
other brassicas needing high fertility.
Harvest: Early types are ready from July to
October: pull when still very small (4cm (1½ins)).
Maincrops are ready to eat fresh, or store in the
autumn, and can be left until ready without

'PURPLE TOP MILAN'

deterioration. They are hardier than the earlies but still need lifting or
protecting in the winter.

Origin and Varieties

Another vegetable that has been around for millennia; the Greeks were partial to
a decent turnip. There are wild forms of turnip found throughout west Asia and
Europe, suggesting that it was selected and bred in many places.
For early sowings, early cultivars must be used like 'Purple Top Milan' or the
pure white-rooted 'Snowball', like a three-dimensional speech bubble.
Maincrops are less common – 'Green Top Scotch' and 'Golden Ball' should be
available.
For just leaves use 'Namenia'.

Pests and Diseases

Flea beetle, slugs, clubroot, powdery mildew

Comments

Hailed by Baldrick (18th century philosopher) as the epitome of culinary
achievement, the turnip is nowadays one of the less celebrated vegetables. Even
television chefs have failed to come up with the definitive turnip recipe.

It is destined, perhaps, to be a minor (also known as 'hidden') ingredient in other dishes: stews and the like. My attempt at stuffed turnip lived up to its name and was stuffed in the compost heap.

The turnip is relatively easy to grow; wouldn't you just know it?

Easily direct-sown, less demanding fertility-wise than its cousins, the leafy brassicas, and ready fairly quickly; 'tis a shame we can't be more positive about the root which isn't even terribly nutritious.

Help is at hand, and we might be looking in the wrong place.

It has been shown that the leaves of the turnip are packed with vitamins and minerals and make a decent salad leaf. All we have to do is collect young, vital leaves, perhaps selectively, as the turnips are growing, or when the root is harvested.

What you do with the root is up to you: grated with carrot and beetroot, maintaining its vitamin C? Turnip chips? Vegetable cricket?

This turnip-leaf phenomenon is so advanced that you can now buy packets of turnipless turnip seed i.e. just the leaves. The most common variety is 'Namenia', occasionally with the honest, yet less attractive tag line: 'turnip tops', alongside.

You can use 'Namenia' in spring and summer along with early varieties of turnips. For salads, cut off the leaves when no more than 15cm (6ins) high), at about 2.5cm (1in) from the ground. If left longer, the larger, older leaves can be used like spinach. No, not put in cans and promoted by a musclebound cartoon sailor.

For early crops of leaves, maincrop root turnips can be left to re-grow the following spring and the leaves cut as above, having been well protected over winter.

Keep turnips with the rest of their tribe (cabbages etc.) in the same block of your rotation. Don't be tempted to include them with carrots, parsnips etc. under the heading of 'Roots', as some marginally less dependable tomes than this recommend.

Turnips are usually considered to be a summer vegetable and can be sown two or three times to give a supply of small, tender roots (and tops). The older and bigger they get, the tougher they will be, particularly with the early varieties. Harvest as required by selecting from amongst the row and carefully pulling.

Herbs

Whilst this is not a herb book, it is quite hard to ignore some plants that are propagated each year for fresh leaves, along the same lines as, say, spinach or rocket. The only real difference is the quantity of leaves we harvest at any one time.

We are not concerned with perennial plants here, therefore many herbs like rosemary, marjoram and sage are excluded. That is not to say we shouldn't have these in our vegetable area – quite the opposite. In fact some of the best vegetable gardens are a mixture of perennial herbs, flowers, fruit bushes and trees with annual vegetables grown amongst and around them. It makes planning trickier and the physical operations of sowing, harvesting, etc. marginally more challenging, but it is well worth it.

Anyway, the three herbs here should be quite familiar.

Basil

Ocimum basilicum
(*Ocimum*, from Greek *okimon* for basil; *basilicum*, basil)
Family: LAMIACEAE

Sowing
When: April
Where: Indoors in pots or modules (cells).
How: Keep warm to germinate (~15-20°C).

Transplanting
When: End of May/beginning of June if going outside.
Where: In containers or in a very well-protected space in the vegetable patch.
Fertility: Medium requirement.
Harvest: Keep pinching out the tops to harvest leaves.

A BIT OF SWEET BASIL
- DEFINITELY NOT FAWLTY

Origins and Varieties
Basil is from Asia and the eastern Mediterranean, and has been cultivated for over 5000 years. That is long enough to have allowed a whole range of varieties to be developed, with variations in leaf (the 'ruffles' types with large, crinkly leaves), colour (purple basils are very popular) and flavour (there are lemon and cinnamon varieties).

For starting out, use the simple, reliable Sweet Basil.

88

Pests and Diseases
Slugs, aphids, damping off.

Comments
Basil is a member of the mint family and shows this with its square, hairy stems. There is also an element of mint, along with a bit of cloves, in the flavour. Reminiscent of carrots, the botanical name of basil actually means 'Basil basil'. Strictly speaking, basil shouldn't be in this book. It won't grow well in the vegetable patch unless it is very sheltered and warm. It is more suited to pots inside, or just outside the house where you can keep an eye on it and protect it. Polytunnels and greenhouses are ideal but out of our scope.

For what is quite a pungent plant, basil is amazingly attractive to slugs, another reason for not growing in the open ground. If it is to go outside, whatever the location, wait until all risk of frost has passed. One solution, weather permitting, is, to grow it in a hanging basket.

Watering should be in the morning and be sparing – basil dislikes the cold, wet conditions that are more likely if watering is in the evening.

A key point for basil-growing is picking it. You nincompoop, I hear you say, the *whole* point of growing basil is to pick it. Aha, I retort, but the emphasis is on keeping picking leaves from the tips to make it bushy and productive and to stop it flowering, and please don't call me a nincompoop. If basil is allowed to flower then the leaves have a less pleasant flavour.

When I am teaching, I have yet to be able to say the word 'basil' without it being repeated back to me in the voice of Sybil Fawlty, the second syllable usually being an accurate octave higher than the first.

Coriander Leaf
Coriandrum sativum
(*Coriandrum*, from Greek for coriander; *sativum*, cultivated)
Family: APIACEAE

Sowing and Planting

When: Early spring to late autumn.

Where: Direct outside, preferably in the carrot block of the rotation. Thin to about 5cm (2ins) apart. It can be sown in modules/cells but not in trays: coriander doesn't like root disturbance.

Fertility: Low to medium requirement.

Harvest: Pick young leaves as required, when they are about 10cm (4ins) long. An alternative is to cut all the leaves off a plant in one go for it to re-grow ('clearcutting').

SLIGHTLY WILTED
CORIANDER

Origins and Varieties

Coriander is native to South West Asia and North East Africa and has been cultivated for at least 3000 years. The Greek name for coriander, *Koriandron*, giving us the botanical name, originates from a resemblance of the smell of the coriander seed to that of a bed bug, *Koris*. Just thought you'd like to know that. For coriander leaf, as opposed to seed, choose 'Cilantro', 'Leisure' or for finely cut leaves, 'Confetti'.

Pests and Diseases

Very little – possibly greenfly (aphids).

Comments

Coriander, or if you are from the Bristol area, coriandle, has similar issues to fennel. One such issue is that there are two versions of it: one for seed, one for leaves.

We are interested here in the wonderful, pungent leaves that can be used in curries, salads, etc. The only problem is that the leafy type quite often wants to be the seedy type. How do we deal with this Jekyll and Hyde of the vegetable plot?

Firstly, sow a type that produces lots of leaves and is slow to bolt.

Next, sow it on a regular basis throughout the year, accepting that at certain times you'll only get a few leaves before it flowers (don't forget, you can still use the resulting seeds).

Avoid stressing the plants – if they get upset they trip into reproductive mode straight away. Stress could come from trying to transplant young plants in a way that disturbs the tap root. The most common stress comes from hot, dry conditions. It makes sense, therefore, to grow coriander at a time of year when it is cooler. September is made for coriander. By getting it to a good size then, you'll have leaves on and off throughout the winter until it flowers in spring. This is best achieved by growing it in a sheltered place – this may be hard to find in an open vegetable plot without cloches. However, it can be grown well in containers.

Some extra and slightly relevant information is that the population can be divided into people who like coriander and people who are abnormal. The latter group have some smell receptors which are different to the mainstream set meaning that they say that coriander tastes soapy. Despite being only 10 to 20% of the population, they also have an extra gene which makes them louder than everyone else so you tend to know about their problem.

Seriously, and marginally less rude, if something you are about to eat is going to be completely spoiled by one ingredient, it makes sense to say something about it. Apparently, there is also a significant group who have unaffected smell receptors yet still don't like coriander. Those are ones for whom therapy might be useful.

Parsley

Petroselinum crispum
(*Petroselinum*, from Greek *petro* (rock) and *selinon* (parsley)
meaning wild parsley; *crispum*, finely curled)
Family: APIACEAE

Sowing and Planting

When: March/April and July/August

Where: Sow indoors in pots or modules
(cells) or directly in the ground. Plant or thin to
15cm (6ins) apart. It should be included in the
carrot part of the rotation. Parsley can be
grown in containers but it has a large tap root
and a high moisture requirement so be
generous with the size of pot and your
watering.

GRITTY
PARSLEY ?   or   BORING
PARSLEY ?

Fertility: Low to medium requirement.

Harvest: Pick leaves as required. If not used fresh, parsley is far better frozen
than dried. It's not a bad idea to chop it fine and then freeze, maybe using an
ice cube tray to make neat, small portions.

Origins and Varieties

Apparently, parsley is the most widely-cultivated herb in Europe. It has had
plenty of time to become so – the curly version was first mentioned in Roman
times.

There are various varieties of both curled parsley e.g. Champion Moss Curled
and flat-leaved parsley e.g. Italian Giant. In recent years the Italian/French-style
flat leaf variety seems to have become more popular than the more traditionally
English, curled type, which has a stronger flavour. This is, no doubt, due to
influence of food writers who think anything continental must, by definition, be
better.

Pests and Diseases

Slugs on young plants.

Comments

This herb, like its close relatives carrot and parsnip, is biennial. This means it
grows and is productive one year and then flowers and is pretty useless the next.
It dies after setting seed in that second year (usually).

Sowing can be in spring or late summer, to produce leaves in summer/autumn
and winter/spring respectively. Flat-leaved parsley is tougher and may keep
going from a single March sowing.

Germination is slow, with some books quoting up to six weeks. The second sowing is quicker, benefiting from the warmer time outdoors. You will be thrilled to hear that soaking in urine overnight reputedly reduces the germination time, perhaps to a couple of weeks.

Why should we grow the curled parsley instead of that tougher, flat-leaved type? Some people reckon the curly leaves have a better flavour and make a dish more interesting. Certainly, flat-leaved parsley doesn't look very special. Also, if you don't use the curled type, how would you manage to trap all of those little bits of grit that make a mixed salad so crunchy?

There is a further, slightly more serious difference.

Parsley is commonly praised for the range and quantity of minerals and vitamins it holds. It also contains an alkaloid called apiol. This is related to the substance in green potatoes that can make us feel unwell. In fact, parsley can cause abortion and can damage the liver and kidneys if eaten in (very) large quantities. This is possibly the reason why it has remained as a garnish rather than a main dish.

You've waited long enough: curled parsley has less apiol than flat-leaved parsley, though more of a dubious psychedelic drug called myristicin (apparently).

Less Common Vegetables and Why You Shouldn't Grow Them

Whilst the title is slightly negative, don't be put off. Trying things you've never grown before can be terrific fun. Plus, for example, I know people who love cucamelons. Admittedly, they are the same people who worry that if they cycled too far into Cornwall they'd fall off the edge of the earth, but each to their own. All I'm doing is pointing out the occasional major drawback. Maybe that's why they're not very common.

They are all annuals or are grown as annuals, so should fit into your rotation somewhere.

Asparagus Pea

Lotus tetragonolobus

(*Lotus,* classical Latin for a wide group of plants; *tetragonolobus,* four lobes)

Family: PAPILIONACEAE

Sowing Directly

When: May.

Where: Directly in a prepared bed 2.5-4cm (1-1½ins) deep.

How: Seeds spaced at 30cm (12ins) in all directions.

Sowing and Transplanting

When: April.

Where: In modules, one seed per cell.

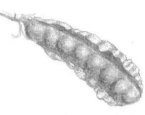

AN ASPARAGUS PEA POD, A BIT PAST IT

How: Push a seed into a cell's unfirmed compost. Transplant to 30cm (12ins) between plants in all directions in May.

Fertility: Low.

Harvest: June to August. Continually pick pods when they are young – 2.5-5cm (1-2ins).

Origin and Varieties

It originates from Sicily.

Pests and Diseases

Slugs, pigeons.

Comments

A strange little pod with wings running the length of it. It is almost worth growing this for the lovely deep red flower alone. It copes with quite a poor soil (free-draining, low nutrients) but will grow better if given slightly more attention, plus lots of sun, as you would expect from Sicily.

The negatives here include a low yield and you have to keep on top of the picking or they become stringy / tough / gristly.

Gerard grew it in the 16th century so the fact that hardly anyone has heard of it since suggests those negatives are too negative.

Aubergine

(Solanum melongena)

(Solanum, classical Latin for the nightshades; *melongena*, either an old name for the egg plant or corrupted Latin for 'mad apple' which is far more fun)

Family: SOLANACEAE

Sowing

When: April.

Where: In cells.

How: One seed per cell, placed in a warm place 15-20°C ideally. Still indoors, pot up the seedlings into 9cm (3 ins) pots when they have two true leaves.

Planting

When: Plant outside in late May–early June when the plants are as big as possible. Harden off first. Space about 45-60cm (1½-2ft) apart.

Fertility: High. Try comfrey liquid every fortnight when in full growth.

Harvest: Tricky one this. Principally when the full colour has been reached and then when there is a small amount of 'give' as the bottom end is pressed. There is an incentive not to let them get over-ripe: they get more bitter.

Origins

Probably from China, not making it to the UK for a couple of millennia. Lots of shapes, sizes and colours. 'Long Purple' is reliable (and over 100 years-old); 'Short Tom' is smaller and early, ideal for containers and 'Violette di Firenze' is strange (skinny, pinky-purple fruits).

A LONG
PURPLE
AUBERGINE
'LONG
PURPLE'

Pests and Diseases

One good thing about trying to grow these outside is there are certain hothouse pests which are avoided. Unfortunately, there are replacement problems waiting such as grey mould / botrytis and slugs.

Comments

My 19th century gardening books don't give it a single mention. It staggers into a 1910 edition of Cassell's with the phrase 'Egg plant, from France where it is called 'Aubergine'.

Nowadays, this is a popular vegetable in our diets. It wasn't long ago that I thought moussaka was a dance, and baba ganoush was one of those Rolls-Royce-driving gurus. It is, however, not a commonly grown plant in the UK, certainly not outside. In fact, don't bother unless you can contrive to improve the conditions over and above the traditional UK summer. Hence, it is sitting in this section of the book.

They are treated very much like outdoor tomatoes with feeding and watering. They do, however, need lots of sun and reliable, elevated temperatures, the latter achieved by either growing in a sun-trap (perhaps in containers – go for a dwarf variety) or using cloches.......or growing in the southern counties.

We could be being a little optimistic here to suggest that an aubergine plant should be kept more compact by pinching out the tip when the plants are about 25cm (10ins) tall. We might be thinking instead how we can make this plant less compact. In common with a number of highly bred vegetables, huge fruits have been achieved at the expense of the structure which needs supporting. Maybe through naturally stockier growth and smaller fruit, our outdoor aubergines may not need that support.

Callaloo

Amaranthus tricolor

(*Amaranthus,* from Greek for 'everlasting'; *tricolor,* three-coloured)
Family: AMARANTHACEAE

Sowing Directly

When: End of May.

Where: In drills directly in a prepared bed.

How: Directly in rows at 30cm, very thinly. Thin to 15cm (6ins) between plants.

Sowing and Transplanting

When: Early May.

Where: In modules, two seeds per cell, thinning to one. Transplant when 5cm (2ins) tall.

How: In each cell sow two seeds shallowly; thin to one plant on emergence. Transplant to 30cm (12ins) rows and 23-30cm (9-12ins) between plants.

THE TIP OF CALLALOO 'BANGLADESHI DHATA'

Fertility: Medium.

Harvest: Mid-August onwards. Remove young shoots / leaves when big enough. Cutting back the whole plant to ground level and getting it to re-grow works very nicely as long as it hasn't started to flower.

Origin and Varieties

It originates from South-east Asia but has been particularly taken up in the Caribbean and brought to the UK as a result. There are few varieties available, but you might find 'Bangladeshi Dhata' or 'Kerala Red'.

Pests and Diseases

Slugs (when plants are small). That's about it.

Comments

The name 'tricolor' is a little ungenerous, with colours ranging from pale green to dark purple. It is an extremely valuable crop, nutritionally, grown throughout the world apart, it seems, from in this country. Having said that, a nearby allotment plot was once covered end to end with callaloo. The entire crop disappeared overnight in a van to Birmingham. Our lovely local shopkeeper told us that in the Punjab women recovering from childbirth were given a nutritionally complete diet of aubergines, millet and, yes, callaloo (fruit, grain and leaf).

Two main problems afflict callaloo. The need for warmth and the tendency to flower. Follow the sowing times and possibly give a bit of protection if necessary to help with the first of those. For the second, South American (not Jamaican) varieties don't bolt nearly as easily, neither do the varieties already mentioned which have been selected for leaf production.

The leaves have a mild spinachy flavour and can be used in salads when young or older larger leaves can be cooked like spinach. Pick regularly and keep watered.

Provided your neighbours haven't grown related plants such as the ornamental amaranth Love-lies-bleeding (amaranths cross with each other far too easily) you can save the seed for the following year. Your flowering / seeding plants will look rather lovely, too.

Chicories

(*Chicorium* species)
Chicory and Radicchio are *C. intybus* and Endive is *C. endivia*
(*intybus* is from the Latin for wild chicory)
Family: ASTERACEAE

Sowing

When: Late spring for a summer / autumn crop. End of
June-Mid July for a winter crop (plus protection).
Where: Trays or modules
How: Two seeds per cell and thin plants to the strongest
plant. Or sow thinly in a half seed tray and prick out when
they can be handled easily. Plant out 30cm (12ins) in all
directions.
Fertility: Low to medium.
Harvest: Cut whole heads as required. They can 'stand'
longer in the cooler months of autumn and winter,
meaning they don't deteriorate too quickly.

Origin and Varieties

Chicory: 'Sugar Loaf' and for serious forcing / blanching
'Witloof'. Radicchio: 'Rossa di Treviso' and 'Palla
Rossa'. Endive: 'Blonde Full Heart' (broad-leaved /
Batavian type) and 'Wallone' (Frizzy / Curled type).

Pests and Diseases

Not bad. Slugs can take up residence in endives.

THE INNARDS
OF A CHICORY
CHICON

Comments

We have sneaked what appears to be three vegetables into one section, though
they are either the same thing or are treated very similarly. In fact, the names are
interchangeable depending on in which part of Europe you've ended up.
The first two are pretty much the same, just different colours, whereas endive is
composed of finely cut leaves (the frizzy green fright wig appearance) or the
slightly less finely cut leaves of the broad-leaved type.
As the terrific author Joy Larkcom pertinently pointed out, this lot might not be
too popular because of the bitterness. But then bitter is good for you (that's the
sharpness, not dodgy homebrew). Apparently, bitter foods stimulate digestive
enzymes and stomach acid as well as, in *Chicorium*, plenty of fibre to promote
healthy gut bacteria. Apart from a good range and level of vitamins (dependent
on the growing conditions, of course) bitter foods perform liver cleansing,
effectively speeding up the processing of naughty food, especially sugar.

In a temperate climate, it has been said that if we are actually going to eat raw food then it should at least have a warming effect: bitter leaves, spicy leaves, 'hot' leaves.

The only problem is, bitter foods are hard to eat. Here are some ways to get around the problem:

- Choose sweeter varieties (there aren't many).
- Grow them as they are and use them in small quantities mixed in with other, sweeter leaves.
- Grow as a cut-and-come-again seedling crop of young leaves.
- Blanch them: exclude light to make them sweeter and bitter- and unfortunately nutrient-free. Perhaps partially blanched (see Endive below) is the answer.

To achieve the last one, it is easier with the endives which, being relatively flat, lend themselves to having a dinner plate sat on top a week or so before harvest. There is a really quite complicated approach to blanching when growing the witloof type of chicory to develop 'chicons' – those strange white-tinged-with-yellow fat rocket ships. Follow the late spring / early summer sowing and, missing out the even more complicated lifting / storing / forcing in pots indoors version, remove the leaves in late autumn and cover the stumps with a deep layer of sand or sandy soil. This is easier to do in rows so plan accordingly. The blanched chicons will appear from late winter to early spring and they are cut after removing the sand. The downside to this approach is that they are ready only at a certain time; indoor forcing can be done to produce a continuous supply.

Or just harvest dandelion leaves.

Cucamelon

Melothria scabra

(*Melothria*, from the Greek for a different plant; *scabra*, meaning 'rough', so one word completely useless and the second setting the tone of this section)

Family: CUCURBITACEAE

Sowing

When: Late April to May

Where: In cells.

How: One seed per cell, placed in a warm place.

Planting

Plant outside in late May – early June when the plants are about 7.5cm (3ins). They need support so a tipi would be useful. Alternatively, some netting strung between posts. Wherever they are, they need good drainage and a sunny, sheltered position telling us that perhaps it should be indoors and not in this book.

A CUCUMBER DISGUISED AS A GOOSEBERRY

Fertility: Medium, with a little extra liquid feed along the way. Try comfrey liquid.

Harvest: Grape-sized individual fruits should appear within two to three months.

Origins

They come from Mexico to Venezuela where they are a delicacy. Apparently.

Pests and Diseases

Next to no P & D, here, showing what great taste our pathogens and pests have.

Comments

Pinch out the top when the plant has reached 2.5m (8ft) or lower if you can't reach that height.

There are nice common names (Mexican miniature watermelon, Mouse melon) and not so nice names (Mexican sour gherkin, Nasty little thing). Choose the one which accords with your level of enjoyment.

There are a few contradictions with this plant:

It likes plenty of water but is drought tolerant.

It needs no pruning (but you have to remove sideshoots).

'They are easy to grow outside in the UK' – but they are mainly grown indoors.

They have a combined flavour of cucumber and lime – or they are too sharp for most tastes.

Goosefoots

(or should that be Goosefeet?)

(*Chenopodium,* from the Greek for, yes, goose foot.)

Family: AMARANTHACEAE

Named after the shape of the leaf, these plants belong in the Amaranth family and there are plenty of them, including Good King Henry and the (edible) weed Fat Hen. The three crops below are, I admit, borderline for us, but if you want to try something different…...

Giant Goosefoot or Magenta Spreen
Chenopodium giganteum

This has bright green leaves frosted with sparkly pink glitter at the growing point. Kate McEvoy of Real Seeds describes it as salad for three-year-olds. You should resist washing the pink dust off because apparently it contains plenty of calcium and protein. As the botanical (and common) names suggest, it is big (up to 2m (over 6ft)), so you need to find plenty of space and keep picking out the tips to slow it down. There are probably four or five pickings per plant before new plants are needed.

The flavour has been described as having 'earthy tones' and a 'fresh grassy quality' neither of which is really selling it. It is extremely productive and easy to grow with older leaves to use as spinach.

Sow seeds in modules in spring and plant out at about 30cm (12ins) spacing. It's an annual.

The nutrient content is reckoned to be pretty good, but what about that oxalic acid content (see p.75)?

If nothing else, that colour makes a great salad addition and if you collect the seeds it can be used as a green manure, though maybe not the best.

Aztec Spinach or Huauzontle
Chenopodium berlandieri

If magenta spreen is used for salad or spinach, huauzontle is used like broccoli. It is bushier than its cousins and gets to about 1m (3ft). The nutritional content is also great with good levels of vitamins, calcium and phosphorus.

It doesn't have the large terminal flower bud of calabrese, but a smaller version, more like purple sprouting broccoli. When cooked the shoots keep their shape yet become tender.

An annual, sow it in cells / modules at the end of April to plant out in late May – early June. Space them 15cm (6ins) apart in rows 45cm (18ins) apart. Keep watered and fed to maintain productivity.

In case you were wondering, huauzontle (I have trouble not seeing 'horizontal', there) is from pre-Aztec Mexico and the word means 'hairy amaranth'. Great.

Quinoa
Chenopodium quinoa

I thought this was worth including if only to prove that we don't have to be dependent on imported rice or millet for our grains. It is also possibly the most nutritious of the lot. You can, of course, collect the seed from several of this family (including huauzontle) and eat that, but quinoa is the most productive by far.

It is possible to buy the seed (there is a great variety called 'Rainbow') but you could also try using UK-grown seed from a wholefood shop: provided it is fresh it should do perfectly well.

Sow and plant as for huauzontle with the timings, and space them out to fill a bed, perhaps how you would with sweet corn, spacing at 45cm (18ins) apart. From then on, it's not quite a case of sit back and wait because there might be some watering to do and perhaps a feed of comfrey when they are in full flow, but it's not much more than that.

The plants are tall 1.2-1.5m (4-5ft) and in the late summer into the autumn the leaves start yellowing and the heads may colour up too. As the leaves drop, it is time to cut the heads and finish the drying inside (a greenhouse or polytunnel if possible).

Pull off the seeds and separate them from the debris by winnowing: this is usually pouring from one bucket to another with a cross breeze to blow out the debris. You can only do a small amount of winnowing by blowing across the seed yourself before you go all dizzy. Spread the seeds out to finish drying indoors.

Kohl Rabi / Kohlrabi

Brassica oleracea Gongylodes Group
(Gongylodes means 'roundish' in Greek, which is a fair description.)
Family: BRASSICACEAE

Sowing Directly

When: March to August direct.
February and September under cover.
Where: In drills directly in a
prepared bed.
How: Directly in rows at 30cm, very
thinly. Thin to 20cm (8ins) between
plants. Leave closer for smaller
kohlrabi (15cm (6ins)).

A LITTLE SPACESHIP
OF KOHL RABI

Sowing and Transplanting

When: February and September
under cover – can be done other
times, too. Transplant when 5cm
(2ins) tall (about 6 weeks after sowing).
Where: Sow in modules/cells or trays. Final position in a prepared bed.
How: In each cell sow two seeds 1cm (½in) deep; thin to one plant on
emergence. Transplant to 23-30cm (9-12ins) in all directions.
Fertility: Medium, despite being a brassica.
Harvest: 10-12 weeks after sowing (longer for February and September
sowings). Remove alternate plants, starting when they are the size of a table
tennis ball. Nowadays, the new varieties can get quite large and still be tender.

Origin and Varieties

Probably developed in Germany in the 16th century. 'Kolibri' and 'Azur Star'
have purple skins and white flesh. 'Superschmelz' and 'Gigant' are in some
catalogues one and same thing: huge specimens without getting tough.

Pests and Diseases

Slugs (when plants are small). All the other brassica problems but to a lesser
degree.

Comments

It is strange to include a vegetable about which there is lots of confusion i) with
the name, ii) the taste iii) what part of the plant it is you're eating. Not to
mention what to do with the thing.

The varietal name calls it stem turnip and the common name is German for cabbage turnip, yet it is not nearly as closely related to turnip as to the other leafy brassicas – it is in the same genus as turnip (*Brassica*) but it is a selection originating from the wild cabbage, as are kale, broccoli etc..

It is hard to pin down the flavour: you can choose from a selection of other vegetables (and fruit), either individually or in combination – broccoli, turnip, radish, cabbage, cucumber, apple. Suffice it to say, it's different. Whether you *like* it or not is different matter.

The part of the plant that you're eating, annoyingly, isn't the root especially as it is often referred to as a root vegetable. It is a swollen stem, which accounts for those leaves sprouting out of the sides (they wouldn't do that from a root). Imagine eating an extra-swollen, peeled broccoli stem – that's pretty much what you've got in terms of texture and, for some, flavour.

It has been in and around the British Isles for at least 400 years and, after all that time, if most people still haven't heard of it, you might question whether it is ever going to catch on.

Culinarily, it can be steamed, added to a stir-fry, a stew ingredient or eaten raw in a salad, perhaps best grated. Don't forget that the leaves can be eaten like spring greens, too.

New Zealand Spinach

Tetragonia tetragonioides
(*Tetragonia* from the Greek for four angles, referring to the fruit shape)
Family: AIZOACEAE

Sowing

When: May, after last frosts.
Where: Directly in a prepared bed.
How: If possible, soak the seeds for a day before sowing. Station sow 20-25mm (1in) deep, 45cm (18ins) between seeds.
Fertility: Medium.
Harvest: About 6 weeks after sowing, start harvesting by pinching out the tips of shoots. This keeps the plants bushy as well as giving you your first leaves. The youngest bits can be used as a

DOWN-UNDER
SPINACH THE
RIGHT WAY UP

salad. It can be picked all summer and, particularly earlier on, the whole plant can be cut back to rejuvenate it.

Origin and Varieties

No 'French bean' skulduggery here – it really is from New Zealand. It has been grown in the UK for a couple of hundred years. No varieties.

Pests and Diseases

Fairly problem-free.

Comments

A slightly confusing name, botanical one that is, meaning four angles when the leaves have distinctly got three angles. And why the full name of 'Four angles, like four angles'? Stick with 'New Zealand Spinach' which is pretty accurate, both in origin and usage.

The particular value is not so much the nutrient content (it's okay for vitamins C and B6 and superb for K), more for its availability during the summer when traditional spinach is producing nothing apart from flowers. The youngest tender leaves can be salad material but usually it is cooked as spinach. Yes, you can create a green sludge using this, too.

Perhaps the small (compared to some others in this section) drawback is the mildness of its flavour. But it easily makes up for that in its availability even in quite dry spells. It is quite a sprawling plant, so give it that wide spacing. The potential is there to last several years (it is a perennial), but it succumbs to low temperatures so save some seeds to start afresh next year.

Oca

Oxalis tuberosa

(*Oxalis,* from the Greek for 'acid'; *tuberosa,* tuberous)

Family: OXALIDACEAE

Planting

When: End of May.

Where: Directly into a prepared bed.

How: 12.5cm (5ins) deep in rows at 30cm with 30cm (12ins) between tubers.

Fertility: Medium.

Harvest: A long time after planting – about mid-November provided there haven't been any serious ground frosts before then.

THE LARVAL STAGE OF THE OCA

Origin and Varieties

Central / southern Andes. The names of varieties are not nearly as inventive as with other crops, in fact they're descriptions rather than names: for example, 'Orange Oca with Red Eyes' and 'New Zealand Red with Black Eyes'. Fortunately, there is also one called 'Strawberries and Cream'.

Pests and Diseases

Slugs.

Comments

Despite being a perennial herbaceous plant, it is frost sensitive so is treated as an annual in the UK. It produces lots of (slightly unkindly) maggot-shaped tubers which have a lemon flavour. This is due to oxalic acid, for the same reason that sorrel is sharp. There is a choice of colours, including yellow, orange, pink, apricot with red the most common.

The nuisance side of this thing, or one of them, is that for the tubers to start forming, the daylength needs to be less than 9 hours. Frost-sensitivity is another and the oxalic acid is a third.

The issue with the daylength is that you can have the plants there all summer, but it is only in the autumn that tubers grow. It is a race, then, to get them as large a size as possible before the frosts kill the tops off. If that happens earlier in the autumn, then – bad luck. You could try covering them with fleece or the like when the first frosts are forecast. Ground frosts will affect the tubers themselves and they will rot.

So, leave the plants for as long as you can until the tops are affected and then remove. This is straightforward and means you can easily grow them in a no-dig system. This is because as you pull up the plant, the tubers (which grow near the surface), will come up with it.

Clean these little fat grubs as soon as you can because they need to be exposed to sunlight for a week or two. So, spread them out in a greenhouse, polytunnel or sunny window to reduce the levels of oxalic acid. A reminder from the spinach section: oxalic acid binds up calcium and iron so is not good for people with bone or joint issues, or are prone to kidney stones. The tubers end up sweeter as a result of this sun-bathing.

Now all you need to do is treat them like potatoes: store in a cool, dark place. Save some fine specimens for the following year when you can chit them and start all over again.

Let us finish with some possible reasons why it is actually worth growing them. The yield is comparable to early potatoes, they store well, they can be grown in containers making them easier to protect, there are reasonable levels of vitamins and minerals (A, B6 and potassium) and......they are different.

Peppers

(*Capsicum annuum*)
(*Capsicum*, from the Greek 'to bite' – no explanation necessary; *annuum*, of annual duration)
(Sweet pepper Grossum group, Chilli pepper Longum group)
Family: SOLANACEAE

Sowing

When: April
Where: In cells.
How: One seed per cell, placed in a warm place, ideally about 20°C.

AN INNOCENT – LOOKING CAYENNE PEPPER

Planting

Harden off and plant outside in late May – early June when the plants are 7.5-15cm (3-6ins). Find a sheltered corner or use cloches to warm the soil and keep the crop going in a potentially dodgy summer.

Fertility: High. Use compost when planting and / or as a mulch. Comfrey liquid can be used fortnightly.

Harvest: Harvesting green, unripe peppers, whether sweet or chilli, will prolong the cropping period since the change to red (or whatever colour ripe is) can take a few weeks, and will result in a yield loss overall of about a quarter. But the ripe fruit is so much more enjoyable......

Origins

They come from Central and South America. Thin-walled Europe-bred sweet peppers are hardier: try 'Marconi Rossa' or 'Gypsy'. There are a ridiculous number of chillies: 'Hungarian Hot Wax' is sweet and yellow turning red and hot (unfortunately, the heat arrives just *before* the change in colour as my nieces won't let me forget). 'Ring of Fire', slightly worryingly-named archetypal hot red chilli pepper. 'Fairy Lights', loads of small triangular fruits with the colours green, yellow, orange and red all on at the same time, indicating stages of ripeness – lovely.

Pests and Diseases

Slugs, grey mould, aphids.

Comments

Along with aubergines this is not an unusual (fruiting) vegetable, certainly not to eat, but it is less commonly grown outside. Most of our supermarket peppers are grown abroad or in hydroponic systems in huge glasshouses in the UK. It might just be worth trying a sweet or bell pepper on the plot for that reason alone. Chillies lend themselves to growing in pots and a reasonable crop can be achieved keeping those in a sheltered place. They are a little more resilient than sweet peppers so maybe try those first.

Peppers have lots of vitamin C, though it might be easier to obtain via the sweet peppers....

The naming of peppers has been a bit of a mess in the past, especially the chillies. Habanero type may or may not be a different species (*C. chinense*, which isn't from China, and may or may not have been bred from *C. frutescens*). We now have the sweet peppers in one group (Grossum, meaning very large) and chillies in another (Longum, meaning long), both reasonable if unexciting descriptions.

I got into a mess with the word '*annuum*' pointing out to a student that it meant 'annual', which indeed sweet peppers are. Unfortunately, he had kept chilli plants from one year to the next and was suitably unimpressed: chillies are short-lived perennials normally grown as annuals.

And another anomaly to confound students: the fruit is, botanically, a 'berry', as well as being a vegetable.

There have been hot chillies from the start, probably before sweet peppers. George Glenny, in his 'Culture of Fruits and Vegetables' (1878) talks only of drying the fruit after harvest suggesting that these were chillies(?). It was relatively recently that varieties were distributed that went off the (Scoville) scale. One of the first was the Dorset Naga (over 1 million units), developed by Joy and Michael Michaud of Sea Spring Seeds in that county. On the radio, when asked if anyone else was aware of this demon of a chilli, the reply was 'No, just us.....and a few million Bangladeshis.'

Physalis (Cape Gooseberry and Tomatillo)

P. peruviana and *P. ixocarpa*

(*Physalis*, from Greek for 'bladder'; *peruviana*, from Peru; *ixocarpa*, from Latin for 'sticky fruit')

Family: SOLANACEAE

Sowing

When: April to May

Where: In cells with warmth.

How: Two seeds per cell, thin to the strongest.

Planting

Plant outside in late May – early June when the plants are about 7.5cm (3ins). Rotation willing, they need good drainage and plenty of sunshine.

A TOMATILLO BURSTING OUT OF ITS LANTERN

Fertility: Medium, so not as demanding as their cousins, tomatoes.

Harvest: Unusually, the fruit drops off, often before it is fully ripe. So, it can be collected and ripened at home or left to ripen on the ground.

Origins and Varieties

Mexico, Central and Southern America. The Cape gooseberry is sometimes called a 'goldenberry', mainly for marketing, but there is a very good variety called 'Pineapple' with a flavour described as pineapple custard. Varieties of tomatillo seem to focus on the colour: 'Green' and 'Violet'.

Pests and Diseases

Problem-free. Strewth.

Comments

Another two crops for the price of one, in this case it is the use in which they differ. There are more *Physalis*'s such as the Chinese lantern; they all have the same 'bladder' or papery husk surrounding the fruit.

The tomatillo is mostly used for savoury dishes such as salsa, having a flavour like 'tomatoes with added lime juice'. The lime juice thing seems very familiar, with oca and cucamelon benefitting from the comparison, too. The Cape gooseberry is sweet enough to eat raw or to have as stewed fruit.

The only problem is, as with several of our less common vegetables, they are not at their best outside. They succeed when they are grown in a sheltered place, in the south and / or with a 'good' summer.

Some sticks may be needed to support the plants.

For good fruit set, you need cross pollination, translating as needing more than one plant. On the positive side, they are definitely unusual, they are productive and easy to pick / collect and, really, no P & D?

Soya Beans

Glycine max
(*Glycine*, from the Greek for 'sweet')
Family: PAPILIONACEAE

Sowing

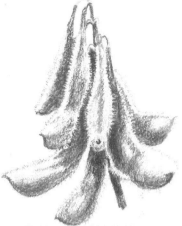

When: Late May
Where: Prepared seed bed.
How: Sow in drills 45cm (18ins) apart with
seeds about 2.5cm (1in) deep and 'thinly' along
the drill. A final spacing of 10cm (4ins)
between plants is aimed for. They can be started
in cells in April and then planted out in late
May, and this may be the best approach for
edamame which would benefit from a wider
spacing in the row (about 15cm (6ins)).
Fertility: Low to medium,

SOME CUDDLY SOYA
BEAN PODS

Harvest: This will be in the autumn for the dried
beans, when the pods have turned yellow. They can be left on the plant to dry
further but you may risk them splitting and dropping the seeds. So, drying
indoors may be an answer. For edamame, harvest like peas, when the pods are
just full.

Origin and Varieties

From China where they have been grown for approximately 13,000 years give
or take a fortnight. For edamame look out for 'Envy' or 'Green shell' and for the
dried beans try 'Ustie' or 'Elena'.

Pests and Diseases

Slugs. Grey mould and other fungal diseases where damage has occurred.

Comments

Well, there are not many vegetables which are as controversial as soya beans.
After all, the Amazon rainforest is being cut down to grow them, so perhaps that
issue needs dealing with before any other. Here is the craziest food system that
could ever have been dreamt up by us.

1. Cut down the rainforest, the world's lungs and habitat to untold numbers
   of creatures.
2. Plant soya beans which have been genetically modified.
3. Use herbicides (glyphosate) and pesticides so that nothing else lives apart
   from soya beans.
4. The beans are harvested and transported hundreds of miles.
5. They are fed to animals which would normally eat grass and herbs.

6. The animals are kept in American 'feedlots' in their millions where they suffer and are slaughtered.
To feed us.

Instead, perhaps we could grow far smaller acreages, locally, of soya beans and eat them ourselves. The soya bean varieties we can grow have low oil content, cook more easily and have a better flavour than those animal-feed commercial versions. Much of the soya for human consumption in this country has been grown in Europe and can easily be grown in the UK following much the same procedure as French beans. Sow with warmth in May (indoors in small pots / modules) and transplant 15cm (12") apart in rows 45cm (18") apart. Shelter, sun and warmth will help enormously.

What makes soya beans a superfood?
High protein levels. All the amino acids required for humans are there.
High vitamin content.
High levels of certain minerals, especially calcium and iron (25% RDA from half a cup).
High levels of insoluble fibre, insoluble and invaluable for feeding the gut flora.
Of the fat, 7% is omega-3.
They contain phytoestrogens which can reduce levels of breast and prostate cancer. There are many other health benefits attributed to soya beans we haven't got time for here.

Despite being incredibly versatile in how they can be used (including tempeh, fake meats, etc.) most of us aren't going to be bubbling up tofu and soya milk on a regular basis. However, one of the simplest and loveliest dishes is edamame where soya bean pods are picked and cooked whole. Sprinkle a little salt on if you fancy and pop out the rather splendid beans.
Growing for the dried beans is slightly tedious in that there are only around three seeds per pod. The huge number of pods per plant sort of makes up for it. Incidentally, the same issues befall chickpeas and lentils. For that reason, it is not worth growing lentils unless you just happen to have threshing equipment to make the separating easy. Try a few chickpeas if only to experience the joy of fresh 'peas' – they are crunchy and nutty and can be eaten straight off the plant.

Sweet Potatoes
Ipomoea batatas
(*Ipomoea* Gk. For 'like a worm or bindweed' depending on your translator and
batatas from the Carib native for the sweet potato)
Family: CONVOLVULACEAE

Propagation
When: February to March.
Where: Organic tubers (to avoid shoot suppressants) are set
on their side, half buried in a shallow pot of cuttings
compost. One tuber can produce half a dozen shoots.
How: Keep the pot in a warm place to encourage shoots to
form. When they are 15-30cm (6-12ins) long, detach
carefully and, if roots have formed at the base, pot up into
9cm (3½ins) pots. If there are no roots, treat the 'slip' as a
softwood cutting: make holes in gritty compost around the
edge of a pot and introduce the cuttings, place in a
propagator or cover with a plastic bag and keep in a warm
place. You may manage to get roots to form in a jar of water.

THE FINE FIGURE OF A SWEET POTATO

Planting
When: End of May / beginning of June.
Where: Fertile, deep beds warmed with a cloche.
How: Ideally leave the cloche on for at least a couple of
weeks or until the weather is reliably warm. Black plastic is
often used to warm the soil (this is unnecessary if using a
cloche) but it also stops the 'vines' – long straggly stems – from rooting in all
over the place. Either plant deeply down the middle of a 1.2m (4ft) bed at a
spacing of 30cm (12ins) or plant in a zigzag 90cm (3ft) apart.
Fertility: High. Perhaps liquid feed with comfrey during growing.
Harvest: Four to five months after planting, usually September into October.
Wait until the leaves start to yellow. The tubers can be quite deep (and vertical).

Origin and Varieties
Orange-fleshed sweet potatoes are probably the tastiest, nutritious and sweet.
'Beauregard Improved' is a version of a well-established, good-flavoured variety
apparently like supermarket varieties, which seems like a good reason not to
grow it. That's not just supermarket-ist, growing your own is chance to try
something different. 'Carolina Ruby' has a red skin and rich orange flesh, well
suited to the UK.

Pests and Diseases
Mostly problem-free. Ubiquitous slugs. Rots of the tubers. Two-spotted spider
mite and whitefly under cover.

Comments

Sweet potatoes are still counted as being a bit exotic in this country let alone the growing of them. This is slightly surprising since, here, they pre-date the common potato which received its name from *I. batatas*.

I suppose we have to weigh up the fiddling about with propagation (or cost of slips / plants) and all the other peculiarities of this crop against the excitement and the yield. In the absence of a greenhouse or polytunnel, then the results will be a little bit more variable. But there are other ways that we can help them to succeed, not least a cloche. It is distinctly possible to grow sweet potatoes in a large pot: try three plants in a 45cm (18ins) pot and you could use a compact variety such as 'O'Henry'. The pot can be moved or protected to provide the best conditions as the summer progresses.

Why you might not want to bother:

> Without the use of some protection, you might not get much in return –
>> high summer temperatures are necessary.

> Strange propagation.

> Long growing season.

> Space – the things can spread everywhere.

> Soil disturbance – the tubers can be quite deep.

Reasons to grow sweet potatoes:

> It is extremely good fun (at least once).

> Not the cheapest vegetable to buy.

> Nutritious.

If you start by buying slips or little plants of a particular variety, then save a tuber or two for the following year so that you can grow your own slips.

Perennial Vegetables

These are included in a separate section if only because they need a permanent place on the plot and don't fit into a rotation or anywhere else in this book. Sorry.

The wonderful permaculturist Patrick Whitefield, after concentrating on perennial vegetables for 20 years, decided that instead of low maintenance he wanted high yield. So, he switched to mainly annuals plus a few reliable perennial plants. Some of the ones he hung on to are included here, but not all – I have been a little more critical. Musk mallow, for example, may produce lots of mild-tasting (synonymous with bland / no flavour?) leaves in spring but is there nothing better?

I've also added some perennials which need a little more care and others so that I can be rude about them.

Asparagus (*Asparagus officinalis*) or Sparrowgrass

A great one to start with, needing its own permanent bed for over twenty years, so choose a sunny site. So, once set up, you have this wonderful annual supply of succulent spears with a little weeding and feeding in return. No other way will you get asparagus as tasty as this. UK-grown asparagus is pretty good, but it is still at least two days old by the time you buy it – the flavour starts to go from the moment it has been picked. Home-grown is essential.

A SPEAR OF ASPARAGUS LAUNCHING UPWARDS (COMPLETE WITH BEETLE EGGS)

Apparently, gardeners would traditionally plant the one-year-old crowns in three rows, 30cm (12ins) apart and the same between plants. That's one heck of a lot of crowns and quite a dense planting. Personally, I go for a single row down the middle of the bed, allowing plenty of space for them to spread over the years. Crowns are more expensive than seeds, but seeds are more variable and take ages to get to the cropping stage. We are told that all-male varieties ('Cito', 'Franklin', 'Backlim', etc.) are best because they don't form berries which waste resources. Quite possibly, but maybe the birds might like some berries. Traditional varieties include 'Connover's Colossal', 'Martha Washington' and 'Purple Passion'.

Plant each crown on a little mound with the top 10cm (4ins) below the surface. This is sometimes done by digging out a shallow trench and adding compost at the same time. Plant in March to April. The following year don't take any spears and in year two just cut a few spears. This is for about five weeks.

117

In year three, you can extend it to eight weeks. Depending on the season this will be in the months April to June.

Harvesting is with a knife at an angle just below ground level – be careful of neighbouring emerging spears – when the spears are about 15cm (6ins) high. Less than this and, apparently, they are less nutritious. Steam or lightly boil for about three minutes then eat them naked. Some people like to add grease of some kind (olive oil?) and some salt. A commercial grower in Somerset told me that <u>all</u> shoots should be cut, even the thin, fine ones (called 'sprues').

The biggest problems are slugs at the spear stage and asparagus beetle when the plants are in leaf. The small beetle (about 6mm (¼ins) is a colourful red, black and white thing. They lay eggs, starting in May, which are black, narrow and tiny, sticking out from the side of the stems / leaves. The resulting grubs can defoliate plants in numbers. Start by collecting the beetles and taking off-site – cup one hand underneath as you go for them because they have a neat trick of dropping off just as you go to pick them off. Wipe eggs off if you can see them. Collect grubs (fat, greyish black, a little longer than the adults) when you see them as dark blobs amongst the foliage.

Asparagus is a coastal plant so copes with salt to the point that some books recommend applying it. This is a missed opportunity: use that freely-available resource known as urine – some salt, and nutrients too.

One final note, still on the topic of urine, is the sensitive subject of its smell after eating asparagus. Whether you produce the smell or not, or can actually smell it or not (or both or neither) depends on genetics. The smell, if it is there, is the result of the production of a sulphur compound.

Globe Artichoke *(Cynara scolymus)*

Now, this is one could go either way. Let us be positive to start with.

It is a wonderful architectural plant with bold and contrasting silver leaves. You won't eat anything else quite like the 'globe' (you might not want to).

The space it occupies is considerable for the return. They only live for about four years. They are quite particular about needing plenty of summer moisture and corresponding winter drainage. The heads are not the most straightforward to eat.

A HEARTY ARTICHOKE

118

Look out for varieties such as 'Green Globe Improved', 'Violet di Chioggia' and 'Purple Globe' and start them from seed. Buy your seeds from a reliable source since there can be too much variation in some selections. Transplant in spring at a spacing of 75cm (2½ft) between plants. Remove flower buds as soon as you see them from the plants in their first year, and in later years remove small lateral buds to concentrate on the central, larger, tastier specimens.

Remove offsets from the base to produce more plants.

Perhaps the main issue with globe artichokes is the magnetic attraction for aphids of a range of colours and flavours, including black aphid. Dry paintbrush – brush them off.

I'm tempted to include the procedure of cooking and eating here, but there is a limit to the number of trees I want to sacrifice in the production of this book. Just that the flower head has, after cooking, two edible parts: the outer 'scales' are held by the pointy end and scraped between the teeth to remove the basal flesh, and the heart of the bud, below the to-be-discarded fibrous choke.

The cardoon, *Cynara cardunculus*, is a close relative and looks very similar to the artichoke if left. Which it isn't. It is a perennial grown as an annual, for its autumnal blanched leaf stalks.

Horseradish (*Armoracia rusticana*)

I suspect I've only included this because of the name of the cuttings (see below) which is pretty puerile. It is relatively limited in its use, basically as a nasal decongestant: horseradish sauce or wasabi substitute is just about the sum total of my culinary experience. Also, the thing can spread throughout your plot unless you're careful – maybe ensure you eat lots of horseradish sauce to keep it in check.

It is raised by planting pieces of root 20cm (8ins) long, called 'thongs' – see, I told you – in early spring. The tops should be about 5cm (2ins) below the surface and spacing, if you are going for mass production, is about 30cm (12ins) apart. Harvest by digging up roots from the autumn onwards. It is quite hard to kill off, so don't worry about replanting.

Jerusalem Artichoke (*Helianthus tuberosus*)

This is perennial in the same way that potatoes are. We leave behind, or plant, tubers to produce the next crop. In the case of Jerusalem artichokes, we almost rely on missing tubers when we harvest, so that, once selected as an artichoke bed, it stays as such. We tend to have marginally more success when clearing potatoes.

Both this and globe artichokes are in the daisy family, the ASTERACEAE, which includes lettuce, chicory and sunflowers, but very few other vegetables.

Plant in late winter / early spring about 10cm (4ins) deep on heavier soils, deeper on lighter soils, with 30cm (12ins) between plants. The RHS recommend cutting the flowers off to concentrate energy into the tubers and others suggest pinching out the tops when they get to 1m (3ft) high to keep them bushy and less vulnerable to blowing over. One of the pleasures of growing Jerusalem artichokes is that they need next to no attention, so perhaps leave them and enjoy the flowers.

A PARTICULARLY UGLY JERUSALEM ARTICHOKE TUBER

It has been said that they can be planted to edge a plot and act as a windbreak: they then collect the wind and release it again when you eat them. Oh dear. They are, in fact, renowned for producing flatulence; they contain a soluble fibre called inulin which is acted on by bacteria in the colon to release enough methane to power a hot air balloon. Seriously, some inulin is very good for you and a wonderful answer to the problem, retaining the artichoke flavour and providing some inulin but not enough to cause embarrassment, is to grate them and ferment them just like sauerkraut or kimchi.

The vegetable **Yacon** *Smallanthus sonchifolius* is very similar in size, growth, productivity and flatulitic nature. It stays crisp after stir-frying like water chestnuts and has a flavour like a crunchy pear.

Slightly interestingly, the Italian for sunflower is *girasole* and since our artichokes are like tall, but small-flowered sunflowers, we have managed to corrupt that to 'Jerusalem'.

Perennial Kale (*Brassica oleracea* selections)

Now this is a truly wonderful plant. Represented principally by two varieties, 'Daubenton's Kale' and 'Taunton Deane'. Let's start with the drawbacks this time: they can be huge (the plants, not the drawbacks) at 1.5 – 2m (5-6ft) so have you got the space?, plus they are relatively short-lived perennials, often lasting for five or six years. Those are minor quibbles compared to the wonderful supply of nutritious leaves whenever you want them. The obvious time is May and June when the over-wintering kales have finished and any new leaves aren't quite ready yet – the hungry gap.

A YOUNG BIT
OF OLD KALE

I harvest mine using secateurs, cutting back to a young side shoot and then selecting the best leaves from the removed head. This keeps the plant in check to a certain degree. One plant should be enough for any plot holder and a singleton will be easier to protect. It can be attacked by every brassica pest going but shrugs off most of them. Pigeons, however, will happily make a complete mess of things so netting is an unfortunate necessity. Young plants may need slug and snail protection.

A slightly exciting aspect of the perennial kale is its propagation. No seeds here – they rarely flower – it is done via cuttings. How strange is that? Kale cuttings. So, to anticipate your specimen kale's demise, take cuttings by inserting new growth from the ends of branches in pots of multipurpose or cuttings compost. They root very easily.

Onion relatives

There is a considerable range of Alliums which can be left in the ground and harvested for bulbs and / or leaves at certain times, but there are very few that are worth giving the space to. A good example is the Welsh onion, *Allium fistulosum* (the same species as Japanese bunching onions). Superficially, these are great: sow the seed or plant some bulbs and you'll have them around evermore, usually where they have self-sown and you don't want them. You dig them up (not easy – they are quite tenacious) in the winter, exactly the time when all of your stored high-yielding 'annual' onions are available to eat. But then you don't have to replant continually on the treadmill of annual cultivation. Really, if you want oniony leaves or bulbs, a combination of spring onions and normal bulb onions should easily cover it. The exception is *Allium ursinium* or wild garlic / ramsons. It can be grown in the shade underneath fruit bushes, filling an empty space (apart from weeds) so there is nothing to be lost. The leaves could fill a garlic gap when your big(?) bulbs / cloves have finished or are starting to sprout or you want to make a pesto or salad for which only ramsons will do. Start it by scattering seeds over the surface in June / July or by starting off plants first and then planting out randomly at about 30cm (12ins). The smallest negative point is that the plants disappear in the summer, so you are left with a blank canvas again. Perhaps combine it with another plant: Martin Crawford of Forest Gardening fame, suggests using the ground ivy *Glechoma hederacea* (the leaves are used for herb teas).

Sea beet (*Beta vulgaris* subsp. *maritima*)

This is one of Patrick's. It is the perennial version of chard and perpetual spinach and you might ask why bother because both of those can, if sown twice a year, be productive all year round. Maybe the answer is in the question – you don't have to sow it twice a year. Plus, it has a stronger, richer flavour and is at its most prolific in May when we're desperate for fresh leaves. There are few pests and diseases though slugs and snails quite enjoy tucking themselves in at the base of plants. Start from seeds and plant out at 45cm (18ins) spacings.

Sea kale, as the name suggests, is in the brassica family and, being smaller than perennial kale, suffers more from pest attacks unlike sea beet. It is also slightly harder to use, either removing young leaves in spring or blanching them (excluding light in the same way that you might torture a rhubarb plant into giving sweeter pink stalks and yellow leaves). You could eat the roots – starchy and indigestible until boiled – or the flowerheads, a bit like broccoli.

Techniques and Practices
of
Organic
Vegetable Growing

Growing Vegetables Organically

For me, the best reason I can give for growing organically is common sense. A bit lame really, but common sense it is. We know deep down that food should not be grown using chemicals, but things get in the way – like cost (we all want cheap food), large-scale production (which lends itself to sprayed monocultures) and availability (we often want out-of-season vegetables).

Agricultural scientists will often tell you that with vegetable growing it is all a matter of chemistry, so what's the difference? Leaving aside the worrying long-term effects of poisonous pesticides, organic growing, like complementary medicine, is much to do with vitality: vitality of the soil and vitality of the produce, which translates into the vitality of the person eating it.

Like so many things in our scientific culture, vitality is very difficult to define or measure, but that doesn't mean that it doesn't exist; it is still recognisable. Growing your own will inevitably mean a proportion of reject vegetables – that is, vegetables that would be rejected by a supermarket. We can of course still eat them, and should. We value something we have put effort in to grow and I, for one, am not going to waste that one-inch carrot or a wormy apple.

A good part of organic growing is sustainability; a well-used word nowadays but this is closest to its original reference: you minimise the number of external inputs to your growing area, and minimise the losses from the same system. Losses will inevitably include the actual food you grow and take away and eat, unless you return your own body waste to your plot – and for most of us, (unless you happen to have a composting toilet) this might not be so 'convenient'. The only alternative is to find another source of replenishment, albeit less sustainable.

The closer you can get to a fully-sustainable system, the more resilient to the uncertainties associated with outside change you will be; and things are going to change. We can already see the effect of increasing demand on natural resources. It's just a matter of time – 10, 50, 100 years? So, now is maybe the time to start getting prepared.

In practice, it would include not being reliant on chemicals and fertilisers (both, incidentally, are on a steep trajectory of price increase); not having to bring in organic matter (if you depend on it, what happens when that source dries up?); using seeds from your own plants rather than going out and buying them, and so forth. It seems that raising plants organically often produces more robust, hardy, self-reliant specimens. Softer, nitrogen-stuffed transplants, dependent on chemical inputs, can be more vulnerable. In nature, predators will invariably go for the weakest member of the herd; the same is true, so to speak, of plants. For wolves, substitute slugs.

It would also include positives, as opposed to the negatives of not doing this, not doing that: for instance, keeping any plant matter from your space, including weeds, and composting the lot. Also, you can grow your own organic matter – green manure. You can save your own seeds: join with other plot holders and get a good range to share. You can develop your own pest and disease control systems, with mixed plantings and flowers. Nobody is going to check up on you. The only person who will reap the consequences of using quick-fix chemicals, is you.

One of the key long-term effects of organic growing is the gradual building of fertility by the return of high levels of organic matter to the soil, which in turn will also improve the structure of the soil, so that plants can establish easily and be able to cope when weather and predators start to threaten. Maybe the mineral and vitamin levels in the vegetables you grow and eat will also increase.

It will take time. Don't forget that our soils have been abused for decades now and for them to recover will be a gradual process.

Last but not least, look to creating a supportive environment system for your space as far as possible, with native trees, shrubs and herbaceous plants that encourage and support wildlife. Grow fruit, herbs, perennial vegetables, comfrey: plants that build a relationship with the soil and the area. Become a gardener who is friendly towards your environment: work with and for nature. Perhaps the most important thing of all is that you enjoy it – which seems to be a widespread feature of organic growers. If you do, you will do it well.

Soil

Your soil is a mixture of things. Commonly, there will be a little organic matter and the rest of the solids will be particles originating from rock.

There are three particle sizes, namely: sand, silt and clay, in decreasing order of size. Yes, clay is the smallest.

Fairly equal proportions of these three gives a soil called medium loam, which is much coveted, especially by me. However, in most of our soils one of the particles is dominant.

The properties of any soil will be dictated considerably by the dominant particles. A clay loam will therefore be 'heavy': harder to work, easy to damage, wet and sticky or dry and cracking. But it will hold water and nutrients well.

SOIL WITH A HIGH CLAY CONTENT

A soil with lots of sand in it – a sandy loam, perhaps – will be the opposite: light, quick to warm in spring, easy to work and harder to damage, but won't retain water and nutrients.

A soil with lots of silt (the third and final particle size) is somewhere in between: easy to damage and holds water well, but not good at retaining nutrients.

You have just wasted several minutes of your life reading information that you don't need. This is because no matter what your soil type, it would be improved by … ORGANIC MATTER. It's in capital letters to make me feel happy and to emphasise its importance as a cure-all for all conditions: heavy soils, light soils, athlete's foot ...

With regular applications of organic matter, a soil with lots of clay in will become more free-draining. A sandy soil is made more moisture- and nutrient retentive with organic matter.

Actually, there are times when it is useful to know your soil type. For example, if you were making beds, it is common to build them up, sometimes with containing wooden surrounds, known as raised beds. They are not the panacea they are sometimes held up to be. They are better for some soil conditions than others. For example, you might not want to do this if your soil is very light, i.e. has lots of sand, since this will make it too free-draining even with organic matter added. The result will be you running around with a watering can as soon as the sun comes out. If you have a heavy soil, a raised bed may help. It would also be a good reason to adopt a no-dig approach, since a soil with lots of clay is pretty hard work and you have to get the timing just right when digging it.

Acid/Alkaline (pH)

Your soil will have a particular pH. This is an indicator of whether your soil is acid or alkaline, or somewhere in between. Neutral pH is 7, acid is below this: 0 to 7, and alkaline above it: 7 to 14.

Well, this is all very tedious, but your vegetables will prefer a particular pH, and if your soil doesn't have it then it might need attention. The ideal pH for most vegetables is slightly acidic, 6.5. Potatoes would prefer it slightly lower and the cabbage family slightly higher, so aiming for around neutral makes sense.

The usual problem with soils is that they are too acidic. This is the case mainly, but not exclusively, with lighter soils. You might need to add some ground limestone. How much you should apply depends on your soil type and how low the pH is. For example, to raise the pH from 5.5 to 6.5 you should apply about 130g/sq. m, if the soil has a high level of sand, but twice that if clay is the dominant particle.

All you need to do is discover your soil's pH. Here are three strategies:

Ask your neighbours what they've been doing all these years (about liming, that is).

Buy a small pH testing kit complete with instructions and liming recommendations.

Alternatively, ignore it all and just get on with growing your vegetables, dealing with any consequences as they arise.

Soil Fertility

Even a twerp like me can deduce that if you take away from a plot by way of vegetation such as crops and weeds, then you have to replace the nutrients that have been lost from the soil. The tricky bit is sorting out what, how much and when.

What to Use

To maintain soil fertility you need to apply either a fertiliser or organic matter. The difference is that fertiliser is a concentrated substance applied by the handful; organic matter is a bulky substance applied by the barrowful. Both, unlike chemical fertilisers, should release plant nutrients slowly, as they are broken down by soil organisms.

Organic matter

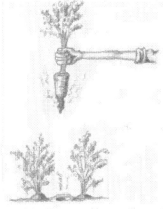

This is by far the best way to supply nutrients since it brings in so much more than fertility. The king of organic matter is homemade compost (see the chapter on Composting). Its only drawback is quantity: can you make enough to maintain your plot? If not then you may need to buy in one of the following, all of which vary in origin, quality and content:

TOO MUCH SOLUBLE FERTILISER CAN BURN ROOTS

Animal Manures

These are either: farmyard manure, which is cow manure, usually mixed with straw; horse manure, which is mixed with straw or, increasingly, wood shavings; poultry/bird manures, which are also mixed with bedding material, but are still quite powerful; so use them with care.

The issue with manures is their source: have those horses been treated with chemical wormers? Has that farmyard manure been contaminated with herbicides?

Ideally, get hold of manure from an organic farm; if not, find out the inputs. This is really important, especially with farmyard manure. Growers have been known to lose a year's worth of crops from weedkillers such as aminopyralid or clopyralid remaining in manure that has then been applied to their soil. Non-organic horse manure should be composted for at least 6 months.

Green Waste Compost

This is made by companies and local councils from garden waste such as prunings, weeds, etc., and sometimes from food waste. It is shredded and composted at high temperatures, making it a 'clean' product. But, in the end, it may contain a high proportion of wood or even bits of plastic. When buying green waste compost try to get a fine grade that has had the larger undecomposed wood chips sieved out.

Leaf Mould

This is fantastic stuff for improving the soil structure and it is easy to make yourself. Its down side includes the time it takes to produce, which is at least a year, and its low nutrient content. How quickly it forms depends on the species of tree the leaves have come from: oak leaves, for example, are more resistant to decay and take longer to break down.

Still, it is well worth getting out of the house and raking up those drain-blocking leaves, stuffing them into bags and leaving them for a year or so: a good stomach-muscle-toning activity. If you want to sweep it up from the street beware of cigarette ends, especially with filter tips. With permission, your local park is often a good source.

Mushroom Compost

This is most commonly horse manure that has been composted, had lime added, and a crop of mushrooms grown on it. Non-organic mushroom compost often has high levels of chemical residues left over from growing the mushrooms and I strongly recommend using only organic mushroom compost. Don't forget that the added lime will, in some degree, raise the pH of your soil.

Organic Fertilisers

With the exception of a few that are derived from ground-up rocks, like rock phosphate, organic fertilisers come from living organisms, and are dried and made into a powder or pellets. Plant-based ones, like sugar beet waste pellets and the truly wonderful seaweed meal (a powder), are perhaps the most acceptable. Over the years, a lot of our nutrients have been washed out to sea, so it makes sense to reclaim some in the renewable form of seaweed; a plant grown using that should contain plenty of trace elements.

If you are a meat eater you will have no problem using some of the abattoir waste products like blood, fish and bone (an all-purpose fertiliser), hoof and horn (good levels of nitrogen to encourage leaf and shoot growth) or bone meal (high in phosphorus to promote good root growth), etc.

Also, slightly confusingly, there are concentrated manures, like chicken pellets, that can be applied as a fertiliser.

Perhaps the most sustainable product of the lot is human-waste pellets. Manufactured by water companies, the sewage is dried, heated, rendered harmless and made acceptable to even the most squeamish of us. The latter completes a circle of sorts, though you could of course short-circuit this process and collect your own...

Another alternative to some of the usual organic fertilisers is rock dust. It comes from quarries where the rock is of volcanic origin and has a naturally high level of nutrients. Ground up, or separated as a powder, it will slowly break down in your soil, providing long-term fertility. Some lucky blighters have soil based on rock like this, such as the volcanic rock soils of the Canaries. But then you'd have to live there to make use of them.

The good news is that it is quite often a waste product. The less-than-perfect news is that it is bloomin' heavy and expensive to transport.

Pure wood ash is also a valuable fertiliser, being particularly high in potassium (potash). However, it has some drawbacks. Used regularly on the same piece of ground, wood ash can affect the soil structure (making a clayey soil stickier) and raise the pH of the soil making it less suitable for some vegetables like potatoes. Maybe it is best used around fruit trees or put on the compost heap.

In a little group of their own are liquid fertilisers. These are used where you have not managed to supply enough nutrients initially to sustain growth for the life of a crop. A good example is tomatoes, where it is sometimes necessary to give a diluted feed each week, one that is high in the fruit-promoting element potassium. Also, of course, it is popular to use liquid fertilisers to keep containerised plants going. Liquid seaweed is particularly good.

It is possible to produce home-made liquid fertiliser (known as teas) by steeping plants in water – anything will do – though nothing comes close to comfrey in terms of the nutrients supplied. Not even nettles can compare to it, mainly because comfrey's strong, deep tap roots bring up nutrients that are out of the reach of most other plants. (See the section on comfrey at the end of this chapter).

One drawback of plant teas is the smell – nettle tea can stun an ox at 20 paces. The liquid produced from wormeries can be used for most plants, since it has a range of nutrients.

How much to apply

This is one of the more difficult things to sort out. Farmers have calculation methods based on soil types, previous crops, next crops, weather, and the fertilisers to be used; plus they employ soil testing to check nutrient levels. We are unlikely to do much of that and often the only assessment of nutrient requirements is how well our crops do.

The good news is that it is very hard to overdo nutrient levels using organic matter. Figures on quantities vary enormously, but try the following compost applications, based on what crop is to be grown next. For heavy feeders such as potatoes, use 1 to 1½, 10 litre/2 gal. buckets per square metre. With medium feeders like onions use up to 1 bucket, and just ½ bucket per square metre for low feeders. For these, where nutrient supply is less important, we could use leaf mould. Manures have a similar sort of strength to compost.

Organic fertilisers will normally come with application rates on the bag. Comfrey liquid is watered around plants once a week in the growing season, provided a good helping of compost was applied at planting.

When to apply

Because most plant growth takes place in the late spring, summer and early autumn it makes sense to plan for nutrient supply then.

Some folk like to plan the year before by spreading manure or compost in the autumn. This is fine, except nutrients may be lost by heavy winter rains, especially on light soils, which can't bind nutrients.

Maybe a better approach is to allow seedlings to commence growth, using the resources in their seeds and the residual nutrients in the soil, and to then apply well-broken-down organic matter as a mulch. Some nutrients will be available from this straight away, and the rest will be released as it continues to break down and gets taken down into the soil by worms.

Another benefit from this approach is that the mulch will act as a weed suppressant when the vegetables need it most, as well as trapping moisture in the soil. However, it can be a little fiddly trying to get compost between the rows of little seedlings.

Fertilisers should be used in a similar way – in anticipation. Remember dry organic fertilisers are often slow release, whilst liquid fertilisers can be applied at any point in the growing season.

There is a fascinating theory, propagated by Dr. Elaine Ingham of the US of A, that a soil with a reasonable clay content will have all the nutrients required for cropping for many years without adding extra. The only problem is that those nutrients are inaccessible to plants meaning you must adopt techniques which encourage micro-organisms which can do that for you. Organic-No-dig anyone?

Comfrey

As mentioned previously, a favourite of mine is comfrey (*Symphytum* x *uplandicum* 'Bocking 14'). This plant was selected for its qualities by gardening legend Lawrence D. Hills, as far back as the 1950's, as the best liquid fertiliser of any tested. The plant is a hybrid and doesn't spread by seed. However, once planted the deep roots mean it is hard to get rid of, if you should change your mind.

Siting and Planting

Prefers full sun and deep soil, but it will tolerate a wide range of conditions including some shade.

Plant pieces of root 5cm/2" deep and 60-90cm (2-3ft) apart.

Preferable times of planting are March to May, or September.

The number of plants depends on the size of the plot and your requirements. For an average full-size allotment a rough guide is 15-20 plants.

Maintenance

Water regularly, especially in the growing season. Ironically, comfrey needs a little feeding. You could use comfrey liquid but that would be cannibalism. Using manure, compost or organic fertiliser to feed comfrey also seems a bit daft, because they can be used directly as plant food to your crops. One answer may be to plant the comfrey around the compost heap to mop up the nutrients that seep out; though make sure it is not in the way of access to the heap for turning, retrieval of compost etc.

Another excellent solution (excuse the pun) is urine diluted 50:50 and applied only after harvesting your comfrey; more than this and salts can build up within the soil.

Harvesting

Don't cut in the first year after planting, apart from removing flowering stems. Make the first cut when the plant is about 60cm (2ft) high, usually in April, and every 4-5 weeks thereafter.

Don't cut later than September, even though it may continue in leaf into November.

4-5 cuts per year may be made from mature plants; build up to this by the third year.

Use shears or a sickle to take all but the top 5cm (2ins) off.

Uses

The leaves can be used as a mulch in a potato trench, or as an activator in a compost heap; but it is at its best as a tea or a concentrate that you can dilute as required. It has high levels of potassium, so it is excellent for flowering and fruiting plants.

To make comfrey tea, place 6 Kgs (14 lbs) of leaves in a 90 litre (20 gallon) water butt, complete with tap. Fill with water and cover with the lid. After 4-6 weeks, draw off the tea as and when required, using it undiluted.

To make comfrey concentrate, use a large container (min. 25 litres/5 galls) and drill a 4-6mm hole in the bottom. Place a narrow-necked collecting vessel under the hole. Stuff with comfrey leaves and cover with a lid. After 7-10 days, dark brown liquid should start dripping into the collector. Comfrey leaves can be continually added to the container as the level sinks. 18 plants can produce 5 litres (1 gall) of concentrate.

Store concentrate in a cool and dark place until required (preferably in the same season it was created) and dilute to between 1:10 and 1:20 before use.

An example is 1:15 dilution, thrice weekly on tomatoes in pots

Rotations – Step by Step

A rotation is a planning system to minimise the build up of soil-borne diseases and some pests, and to maximise the use of nutrients in the soil. Such is its importance that in order to be certified as an organic grower by the Soil Association (for example), you must use a rotation. Whether you do or not, will depend on how much space you have, and whether you can be bothered.

A plot is divided up into a number of equal-sized blocks and different families of vegetables, either alone or combined with other families, are assigned to a given block. They should not be returned to that block again for at least another four years. The number of blocks created is the same as the number of years to complete a cycle of the rotation. Four blocks = A four course rotation = A four year rotation. Don't get confused with beds which are little growing spaces of a specific size (usually 1m to 1.25m (3 to 4ft) wide and paths no narrower than 30cm (1ft)), an equal number of which will be fitted into each block.

In fact, a great way of starting is to measure up the plot to see how many *beds* you can fit in. For example, if it was (conveniently) eight, you could decide to have a four-course rotation (two beds in each block) or an eight-course rotation (one bed in each block)

The recommended procedure is as follows:
1. Identify the area to be used for growing annual vegetables, excluding a shed, most fruit bushes, compost heap, etc.
2. Measure it.
3. Draw your plot to scale on a sheet of paper.
4. Draw on your plan how many beds (if you want them) of your chosen size you can fit into the plot – don't forget the paths.
5. Now draw in the blocks, all equal-sized and each containing the same number of beds. It is often said that four blocks – i.e. a four-course rotation – is the minimum. However, to avoid certain persistent diseases like clubroot or white rot, there should be at least eight blocks i.e. it will be eight years before any crop returns to the same space.
6. Make a list of the vegetables you wish to grow and how much of each one you want to grow, as far as possible. For example, you may hate swedes – so don't grow them. Also, you may love potatoes, but they take up a lot of room and organic potatoes are relatively cheap to buy, so perhaps miss them out if you have limited space.
7. Group your chosen vegetables according to their plant families. In rotation terms, anything in the same family can be assigned to the same block. The vegetables in this book are in the following families, together with a guide to how demanding they are in terms of their required fertility.

By following the table below, you can easily see how to group vegetables and organise their planting sequentially:

Family	a.k.a.	Members	Fertility	Latin Family Name
Onion	Alliums	Onions, Garlic, Leeks, Shallots	Medium	ALLIACEAE
Beetroot		Beetroot, Spinach, Chard, Callaloo, Goosefoot	Medium	AMARANTHACEAE
Carrot	Umbellifers	Carrots, Parsnips, Celery, Celeriac, Parsley, Coriander, Fennel	Medium	APIACEAE
Lettuce	Lettuce or Daisy family	Lettuce, Chicory, Salsify, Scorzonera	Low	ASTERACEAE
Cabbage	Brassicas	Cabbage, Calabrese, Cauliflower, Brussels sprouts, Kale, Turnips, Swedes, Radish, Broccoli, Rocket, Kohl rabi	High	BRASSICACEAE
Squash	Cucurbits	Squash, Courgettes (incl. marrows), Cucumbers	High	CUCURBITACEAE
Pea	Legumes	Peas, Broad beans, French beans, Runner beans, Soya beans, Chickpeas, Asparagus peas	Low	PAPILIONACEAE
Sweet corn	Grass family	Sweet corn	High	POACEAE
Potato	Solanums	Potatoes, Tomatoes, Peppers, Aubergines, Physalis	High	SOLANACEAE

8. Fit the families into your chosen rotation, sequencing and grouping them according to fertility needs. Here is an example of an eight course rotation, with their respective fertilities:

Green Manure Low	Potato Family High	Carrot Family Medium	Pea & Bean family Low	Cabbage family High	Onion family Medium	Squash & Sweet corn families High	Beetroot family Medium

Most nutrients would be applied to heavy feeders. The following year, medium feeders will grow where the heavy feeders were e.g. carrots mopping up the nutrients left over from potatoes – the blocks move from right to left. Peas and beans would move to where the carrots were.

9. In the example above there is one block called 'green manure'. Effectively this constitutes a rest period allowing the soil to recover and be improved (see green manures in 'Organic Growing Systems'). Lettuces could be dotted amongst other crops.

Squash and sweet corn families are combined: both are heavy feeders. This is just one way of doing an eight-course rotation. The design is very flexible as long as you try to incorporate as many of the basic principles as you can. Here is a suggestion for a five-course rotation:

Potato, Squash & Sweet corn families High	Carrot and Beetroot families Medium	Pea & Bean & Lettuce families Low	Cabbage family High	Onion family Medium

As before, in year two the families move from right to left with the area where potatoes were grown, used for carrots etc. and so on. The green manure has been sacrificed (shame) and it has been assumed that not many potatoes or tomatoes are to be grown. In this plan, in accordance with my preferences, lots of space has been given to the big brassica family and to the onion family. You may choose differently.

10. On a very small area – less than the size of, say, four beds – you might prefer to forget the rotation and enjoy a great mixture of vegetables in any old position, year after year. It will be hard to plan quantities, but then that area isn't going to feed the 5000 anyway. Concentrate perhaps on some of the quicker-growing vegetables, and ones that look particularly good.

11. Make a few copies of your plan with its blocks and beds and write in what has been grown each year, together with the dates of sowing / planting. This will be a valuable record as you continue to develop your garden.

Basic Tools

This is a list of the basic tools I think are vital when starting off: digging fork, hand trowel, rake and hoe. Others can be added as and when you feel the need, like a spade.

With the first two it is a simple case of getting what you pay for. Cheap forks end up with bent prongs, (or tines as they are properly known) and broken shafts, a lot sooner than the more reliable brands. The most important part with a trowel is the junction between the blade and handle. Because we misuse them for prising up stones, clods of earth etc. (don't try denying it) all of the strain is taken at this point, and bending, if not breaking, is commonly the result. So, best obtain one made from strong rigid steel. The same applies, even more so, for a hand fork.

It is probably safe to get a relatively cheap rake head because it is used much less frequently than a fork or trowel.

The size of the handle is quite important with all tools, and the more you can stand upright when you use any tool, the better your back will be for it. Hence, with a rake or hoe, if you are six foot or over, an extra-long pole should be used; for the fork it is hard, but not impossible, to get extra-long shafts.

The hoe needs a lot more thought. The cheapest, and one I'd heartily recommend, can have any one of three possible names: Dutch hoe, push hoe or stirrup hoe. Take your pick. Sorry, that's a different tool altogether (and an old joke). See the drawing for its appearance.

The key here, as with all hoes, is sharpness: you have a blade on a stick and to be most effective in cutting weeds at or just below soil level, it must be sharp. The angle of the head to the shaft is also important: it is easier to use if the angle is wide (see pictures) since the force you apply goes down the handle and through the blade more efficiently, but too wide an angle will mean you have to hold the handle lower to the ground than is good for your back.

You can try a more expensive hoe, called an oscillating hoe, that is brilliant for clearing large areas. It has a thin piece of metal for its blade so it doesn't need sharpening and it cuts when you pull it as well as push by virtue of a hinge (hence the oscillating bit).

Other useful kit includes string lines, which don't need too much explanation: two pegs or sticks with a length of string joining them. Make it long enough to stretch the length of your longest bed and so, for the perfectionists amongst us, our planting can be in nice, neat, straight lines.

A kind of large hoe, sometimes called an azada, sometimes a Chillington hoe, or occasionally, and incorrectly, a mattock, is apparently the most used tool in the world. It is heavy, has a shortish handle and is used for chopping. It is often used instead of a spade but it is also extremely useful for killing off green manures. Again, it should be kept sharp.

A spade is perhaps more familiar than an azada and may be the preferred choice for confirmed diggers. Sharpen it by running a cigar stone (a tapering abrasive stone about 25cm (10ins) long) over the end.

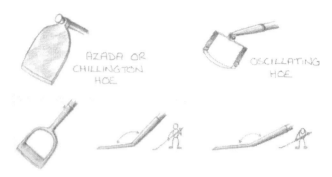

Always remove soil from your tools and place it back onto the beds before storing them. An old paint scraper is exceptionally useful for this. Wipe mud off the handles, if only to make it more pleasant the next time you use them.

Finally, a little advice on how to use tools: if you are bending over to use an implement, first of all try not to if you can possibly help it; this might mean getting a longer handle. Whatever your posture, try to swap hands over after a short while so that, for example, as a right-handed person using a fork your right hand will be on the handle and left hand on the shaft. Swap over so the left hand is at top (see the picture on page 122). The strongest muscles in your body are found in your thighs so use those to push the fork or spade into the ground, not your arms.

Using a fork in a rotating motion to tweak the soil surface and break down surface clods requires your top hand to be under the handle not over the top, as shown. This will reduce the strain on your arm.

It is the same with a hoe or a rake: swap your hands over every few minutes. Your spine will bend in the opposite way to the way you are used to, but it will be exercise for it rather than a strain. It may feel weird, but you'll get used to it.

What to do First On a New Plot

On acquiring a new plot or garden, once the excitement/panic/dread (please delete as appropriate) has subsided, there are a few things to do before touching a spade or fork.

Firstly, note what is there, referring to plant life rather than the shed, an old growbag or the cat. The success of this part depends largely on your knowledge of plants and ability to identify them, and, of course, the time of year.

We are sometimes told to 'live with a piece of land for a year': in other words, see what comes up and thrives. Usually these are weeds. Still, it is sound advice if you have the time and can suppress the desire to get on with it.

What might there be for us to look out for?

On an allotment it could be fruit or perennial vegetables like artichokes, rhubarb or even asparagus. In old grassland it might be wildflowers. In a garden it could be virtually anything. In the winter, much would be hidden below ground.

MAKE SURE THE AREA IS CLEARED BEFORE COVERING

Let us assume that there is nothing of value, there is and you've moved it or you don't care.

The first step is to gain some control. Unless you are lucky and the area has been used recently, there will be a range of weeds covering the soil.

Frequently they are pernicious (seriously undesirable), perennial, spreading things. Here is a short list of possibilities: couch grass, bindweed, brambles, cinquefoil, creeping buttercup, ground elder, horsetail, etc. If it has Japanese knotweed on it, decline the plot or contact your local council – yes, it's that bad. If you don't know what any of these look like, you will need to find a knowledgeable friend or get a book on wildflowers. Sorry.

Next decision: how soon do I want to use this space? All at once, or can it be bit by bit?

Covering the ground will kill these weeds (by excluding light) given enough time; for most this would be a whole growing season. Even if you've decided to use all of the land as soon as possible, still cover it and put it on hold until you are able to do the clearing by hand.

Covering the ground

To begin, cut down and remove any unwanted woody tops like old fruit bushes, brambles, etc.

If you are able to, roughly hoe off any other plants there and even put down some organic matter to help improve the soil. Then lay some kind of light-excluding material over the surface.

You can use black polythene but there are issues surrounding it, like its origin (oil-based product), its disposal (recycling?) and its effect on the organisms in the soil. Certainly, long-term use will reduce the presence of beneficial fungi, etc. However, it is the most effective non-herbicide method.

Landscape fabric will have the same effect but is marginally less detrimental to fungi because it is porous. Beware of leaving a porous material down for too long – weed seeds will land on the surface, germinate and eventually root through it making it fiendishly difficult to remove. Carpet is now banned from most allotment sites partly as a result of this, and partly because of chemicals that can enter the soil.

Cardboard may be a preferable and more sustainable solution. There is a huge amount thrown out by shops. Get the biggest sheets possible, (perhaps by breaking open large boxes) and overlap them by a minimum of 15cm (6ins). It will need weighing down, and this is what makes it look 'orrible – bricks and planks all over the place. If you try using wood chip, bark or the like to cover it, it will look better but best not; it will keep the cardboard wet, soft and so less weed-proof; couch grass, for example, would grow straight through it.

You can buy biodegradable mulches – a black plastic made from corn starch that breaks down in four to eight months, or a paper mulch made from cellulose fibres that is porous and blocks light. They have been designed mainly for commercial use in crop production, not land clearance.

To use the land straight away, you can plant through any of these materials, it being a lot easier to set out, say, squash plants or Brussels sprouts, than to sow a row of carrots.

Alternatively, physically remove weeds from uncovered parts using a fork. An azada (see 'Tools') is very handy for removing bramble roots.

With most of the weeds listed, if you leave a small amount behind it will re-grow so it takes several attempts to clear an area. After the initial weeding, if you want to get on with sowing and growing, just keep the trowel handy for those bits that will pop up amongst your crops.

Beds

As you uncover or start to prepare the ground, this will be a good time to decide whether to have raised beds. If you so decide: firstly, mark out the paths and the beds using stringlines. Try to avoid walking over any of the area too much as the marking out is done.

Paths shouldn't be narrower than 30cm (12ins) and preferably wide enough to take a wheelbarrow. Don't make them too wide, however, or you'll be losing valuable growing space.

The width of the beds should reflect how far you can reach: most are recommended at 1.25m (4ft) but if you are of a shorter stature go for 1.1m (3½ft) or even 90cm (3ft).

Next, work your way along the path, weeding as necessary, and moving a good 15cm (6ins) of topsoil out on to the beds. As you go, walk on the path that has been dug out so that you're not compacting the soil to be moved. The effect of this is to increase the depth of topsoil in the growing area and lower the surrounding paths, thereby increasing the drainage. This is a great benefit, especially if your soil has quite a high content of clay. You will have decided before starting whether to use timber surrounds (old scaffolding

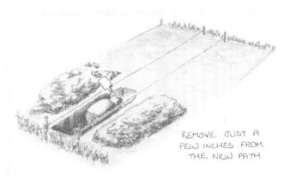

REMOVE JUST A FEW INCHES FROM THE NEW PATH

planks are terrific). Now is the time to knock stakes into to the ground and attach the planks to them. The timber is nailed, or preferably screwed, to them. The stakes should be on the inside, that is the bed side of the timber rather than the path side. You'll see the reason why when you've gone flat on your face for the fourth time in half an hour, tripping over outside stakes.

If you don't use timber to hold back the soil and organic matter you have piled up, then the beds will eventually develop a rounded top and the paths will need an annual scraping (spade, azada) to put back fallen material onto the beds.

An important part of developing a raised-bed system is that the growing area never gets walked on. The amount of work saved in this simple act is huge. Even if you want to regularly dig the beds, you're not having to break up soil compacted by your great clodhoppers.

Planning your rotations and keeping records is so much easier when your growing space is in distinct units. Being better drained will mean the beds will warm up quicker in spring, and you can get going sooner. Make structures like cloches to fit the size of your beds.

Light soils won't benefit from being raised up but having distinct beds and paths will economise on the application of organic matter if nothing else.

Sowing Seeds
in pictures

Seed trays

| Fill | Scrape off | Firm | Sprinkle seed thinly | Cover, scrape off, firm again |

Modules/Cells

| Fill | Scrape off | Firm | Make holes with a pencil |

| Feed seeds into hole | Cover, scrape off | Thin to one seedling per hole |

Nursery Seed Bed

Prepare small area, weed and loosen soil

Put in row markers every 15cm (6ins)

Run stringlines between markers or use a board

| Make a furrow ('drill') with a trowel 1.5cm (½) deep | Sow seed thinly along furrow | Cover | Firm | Water gently | Thin to one plant every 2.5cm (1in) |

Composts for Sowing

The word 'compost' is mildly confusing in this context, since it refers both to the stuff you make in a heap from vegetable peelings etc. and to bags of formulated growing media, e.g. a bag of potting compost bought from the garden centre. Even more confusing is the fact that compost from the heap can be used as an ingredient in your own growing medium. See the homemade compost bit in 'Containers'.

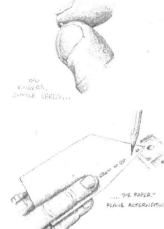

When sowing seeds, you should use either seed compost or multipurpose compost. The latter is formulated so that, in theory, it can be used to sow seeds into it, or for potting up plants. If you can, buy separate bags of Seed and Potting compost. Their difference lies principally in the level of nutrients but often also in the proportions of ingredients. The potting compost is a lot stronger and could inhibit seed germination.

If you buy proper organic seed compost you know it will not have chemical fertilisers added to it and it will not include peat as an ingredient. Unfortunately, there is a loophole in the naming of such products: believe it or not, if they are made from plants they can be called 'organic' (which means originating from living things), even if they contain other non-organic ingredients. Only those which have the symbol from a certifying body, like the Soil Association, will be organic in the sense that they are guaranteed chemical and peat-free.

Where to Sow

Throughout this book you have the recommendation to start off some vegetables 'inside'.

This is because some plants need higher temperatures and/or it is a way of getting plants started sooner, and consequently cropping quicker. If we start them off earlier indoors and plant them out when the conditions are right, we will have earlier crops.

Most of us don't have greenhouses or polytunnels, so we are left with… the windowsill.

Unless you live in an un-insulated caravan, tent or cave, etc. the interior of your accommodation will help enormously, for the simple basic reason that it is warmer. This can be taken a stage further by using a heated propagator: a tray with a built-in heating element and clear plastic lid over the seed trays, to ensure steady warmth. The more expensive ones have thermostats, allowing you to adjust the temperature.

Anyway, with the bold assumption in these straightened times that it is warmer in your house than outside, germination will be quicker and more even on your windowsill (remember to have the curtains drawn between the window and the seed trays on frosty nights).

Surprisingly, it is not the temperature that is the stumbling block. The difficult bit comes when the seedling emerges.

The problem? Light. There is never enough on a windowsill, even one which is south facing. The seedlings bend towards the light *and* get stretched at the same time. The latter is called 'etiolation' and is the hardest to remedy, whereas

HAPPY, TURNED, STROKED SEEDLINGS

A BIT GRUMPY BENT, ETIOLATED SEEDLINGS

bending seedlings can be prevented by regularly turning the trays or modules. Etiolated seedlings are amazingly easy to damage, especially when you come to plant them out: the stems crease and tops die. This is best prevented by increasing light levels; in practice this is not easy.

If it is warm enough outside, they can go out during the day and back in at night. In the spring, however, it is often too inclement. It may be worth investing in one of those little cupboard-like frames with a clear plastic coat. They are cheap and generally slug-proof but are vulnerable to blowing over. Also, remember that they are not heated so it would still involve moving seedlings back into the house when the temperature is low.

Stroking seedlings regularly is supposed to make them stronger, shorter and sturdier. Don't laugh; this is a scientifically proven fact. So there. You might have to do quite a lot of stroking to make it work, though.

I was going to say that providing supplementary lighting is beyond most of us, but if people growing drugs in the attic can manage it then so, arguably, can we. However, buying, fitting and running the special bulbs, known as grow lamps, is expensive. Compared to several bushels of marijuana, an early crop of runner beans may not be as cost-effective.

Composting

There is a definition of a compost heap along the lines of: 'A mound of immovable twigs and nettles at the end of the garden'. We don't want that kind of talk around here.

There is an argument to be made for having the compost heap as the focal point of the garden, and even close to the back door for easy access. It depends if you have a seating area nearby to enjoy the fragrant odours. What is a more practical idea is to have a temporary bin with a lid near the back door, to reduce the frequency with which you have to transfer the kitchen vegetable waste to the more distant compost heap/bin.

Cold Composting

Too often we have information about systems of composting that are either over-complicated or not helpful. The following process is the one most of us will use and is probably the easiest.

We rarely have a lot of material like peelings etc. to compost at any one time. Usually, we add to a heap gradually. The significance of this is that the heap won't heat up and hence it is termed 'cold' (in practice 'ambient' would be better). This in turn dictates what can be put on it or, more to the point, what you shouldn't put on it. If you have lots of plant material available at one time then, wonderful, it will heat up and you will see it steaming like a large rugby player on a winter's day. If you sustain this heat by turning the heap every few days (to maintain the air content) then it will kill nasty things you've put in it; such things as persistent weeds or diseased plants that won't be killed off in our cold heap, from which they should be excluded. Occasionally, like at the end of the season when crops are cleared, there may be a good half a heaps worth of material, and this could heat up a small amount. Don't get too excited – unless you turn it after a few days, this heat is not enough to kill the nasties (which you wouldn't have put on in the first place, would you?). It is still a cold heap.

First step: provide a container, complete with lid or cover. For hot heaps, a series of cubes of one metre dimension is the minimum size and these could be made from pallets. That size would be rather splendid for our miserable cold heap, too, but not essential. In fact, the slightly conical, plastic 'daleks' are fine.

Next, rat-proof it. Buy fairly fine-meshed chicken wire and stand the bin on it. Fold the chicken wire up the outside to about 30cm (1ft) and, if you fancy, tie it in position with string. If you are using pallets you might need to line the whole thing.

Most heaps will lose liquid from the bottom and it usually seeps into the soil. If the heap, including its frame, is moved on a regular basis (e.g. annually), you can make use of this fertilised ground to grow crops. Alternatively, it could be captured and used as a liquid feed elsewhere. One way of collecting compost liquid is to stand your bin on a bit of corrugated sheeting, which is tilted at a slight angle. At the lower end a bit of guttering and a half buried collecting vessel should complete this slightly Heath Robinson affair. The liquid is diluted about 1:10 before using.

Start filling. This is where a little planning is required, not only on what *not* to put in but the combination of ingredients. Avoid the following:

Any animal products

Cooked food

Diseased plants

Perennial weeds like dandelions, couch grass, bindweed, ground elder

Weeds that have flowers and seeds forming

Lots of leaves or lots of any one thing for that matter

Twigs

Synthetic materials, e.g. plastic

NEVER PUT ANIMAL PRODUCTS ON THE COMPOST HEAP

So, what do you do with this lot if you can't compost them? The top three should be sent for council recycling. The cooked food can be put in a wormery, but that is a whole different, yes, can of worms (see p.148).

The perennial weeds have stolen your nutrients and it is your duty to reclaim them – in other words, don't follow the popular route of the bonfire. Instead, dry them out away from the soil during the summer. For the rest of the year when it isn't hot and sunny enough to do this either submerge them in a bucket of water until drowned, or pack them into a robust black bag and leave them for a year at least. Once properly dead, they can then be put on the heap.

Seeding weeds are a nuisance and, look, you just shouldn't have let them get that far in the first place. Oh all right, they *have* got a knack of doing things like flowering, when you're not looking. Being a little obsessive about my soil's nutrients, I spend a little time as I weed, pulling off the flowers/ seedheads. These are dumped in an 'out-of-the-way' place, like a hedge bottom (not my hedge) or the council bin, and the rest is composted.

Compost leaves separately (see 'Leafmould'). It is fine to put a few on the compost heap, but not many in one go.

Twigs should be reduced to small pieces; if you are lucky you may have a shredder, the results then being added to the heap in small amounts. Cutting up twigs with secateurs is possible but tedious. Maybe create a separate, heap of twigs on the longer term, - also known as a wildlife habitat.

One special case is grass cuttings. If you have a large garden then you will end up with plenty of them. Here are a number of solutions: you can reduce the area of lawn (which is often the most time-consuming feature of garden maintenance anyway) preferably by converting a good portion of it to food production. How about developing an area of the lawn into a wildlife meadow, i.e. cut it only a couple of times a year? Also, with a conventional lawn, don't collect the grass cuttings, particularly in the summer because this reduces the need for feeding the lawn and provides organic matter to improve the soil under the lawn. If you still have lots of cuttings then make sure you have plenty of other material to balance it with when it goes into the heap, as with this next bit…

Combination of Ingredients

To avoid the archetypal wet, smelly compost heap you need a good mixture of materials. Ingredients are often described as 'green' (high nitrogen) or 'brown' (high carbon). When gradually building a heap, equal proportions, by volume, of each type should be used. It is common for us to under-use the browns. In other words, you should be putting in more cardboard, paper, fine woodchip and/or shredded prunings and twigs. For most of us, it will be mainly cardboard and paper.

The 'greens' consist of fresh, wet material like peelings, grass cuttings, weeds, etc. Mix them well with the browns as they go in.

If you get the combination right, you'll find a healthy population of brandling /tiger worms building up near the top.

With a plastic bin, that's pretty much it. When you want compost, lift up the bin and set it down in a new place on more chicken wire. Remove the fresh material from the top of the heap left behind and put it in the newly positioned bin. The remaining compost can now be used.

Incidentally, the little door at the bottom of some plastic bins is fairly useless – you can't get compost out very easily without un-rotted material dropping down before you've finished – it's also extremely fiddly.

In a bin with more air around the outside, such as one with a wooden frame, you might decide to turn it to mix the dry, un-decomposed material from around the edges, into the middle.

With any type of compost heap, if you get the proportions wrong, by putting in too much brown material, the compost can end up a little dry. Moisture is essential for decomposition, so add water, or even better, a little dilute urine – one good wee in a half-full watering can should do it. This is easier to perform and less likely to lead to arrest than doing it directly onto the heap. The nitrogen in your urine will also act as an activator and will get the heap going again.

Wormeries

If you have created a cold heap there is a good chance there will be lots of worms on and just under the surface. They seem to find their own way there. This almost makes it a wormery, the difference being that a true wormery is an enclosed structure. The worms can't escape, even if they wanted to.

An example of a homemade wormery would be an old dustbin or wheelie bin with a lid that should let in a little air. Make some small holes around the sides of the lid to be certain. A tap should be fitted close to the base and coarse gravel put in the bottom of the bin to a depth above the level of the tap. This is so that any liquid that drains downwards is captured and you can drain it off to dilute 1:10 and use as an excellent liquid fertiliser.

BRANDLING WORMS MAKING A BREAK FOR IT

On top of the gravel put a small section of landscape fabric, or Hessian sacking, to act as a divider. Next put a helping, about 10cm (4ins), of fresh compost from a heap, complete with a good handful of worms, as a 'starter'. This will also provide the worms with somewhere to live right at the outset. Brandling worms can be bought if you haven't any to start with: about 50-100 are needed initially. Next start adding compost ingredients, which are basically the same as for a cold compost heap with the following exceptions:

Miss out	Add
Citrus	Cooked vegetables
Onion skins	Cooked grains / pasta
Tough shells or fruit stones	Bread
Woodchip	Ground up egg shells

As with any compost heap, it is best to avoid animal products, excepting egg shells; meat putrefies and attracts flies. Still add shredded paper and cardboard, but whatever you put in, do so in small quantities: no more than 5cm (2ins) at any one time. Too much will upset the worms by breaking down via bacteria and even possibly heating up briefly. Cover the surface with a thick layer of damp newspaper.

A wormery can go for a few weeks (the length of your holiday?) without being fed. However, leave the tap open for the liquid to drip out into a collecting vessel rather than build up inside.

Keep your wormery warm if possible:10-30°C is ok, but 18-25°C is ideal for maximum activity. As a result, it should be kept shaded in the summer and insulated in the winter. Some people have them indoors – worms are a lot better than some other pets.

Leaf Mould

Because there are lots of them available all at once (at a time popularly known as autumn), and because they take a while to break down (by fungi rather than bacteria, as in a compost heap), compost leaves by themselves. Either create a wire netting cage of about a metre cubed and stick them in there, or pack them into plastic sacks and leave for a year at least. During that time, they must stay moist – feel free to add a little dilute urine as required. The reason it is so slow is because, in dead leaves, the resources are complex and not readily available to the fungi, like the sugars and starches in kitchen waste, for example. Plus, there are preservatives such as tannins. Plane and chestnut leaves are very slow to break down, with oak not far behind, meaning you may need a couple of years to get the rewards from those.

Good leaf mould is terrific, as an addition to a homemade compost, for sowing seeds. Used as a mulch, it provides little in the way of nutrition. However, it suppresses weeds and holds in moisture, plus it supplies plenty of humus. Humus, wonderful humus: it is responsible for improving the structure of any soil, in the longer term.

Incidentally, hummus or hummous, which is made from chickpeas and olive oil, is rather expensive and should not be used as a mulch.

Why Compost is so Wonderful (and why wormery compost is even better)

It includes all the nutrients that plants need, since it is made from plants in the first place.

It is slow release: nutrients escape from the compounds in organic matter as they are broken down, which happens faster in warmer, moist conditions; exactly those which promote rapid plant growth, so the nutrients keep pace.

It adds to the soil a huge range and quantity of beneficial microorganisms, which aid plant growth in a number of ways.

It improves the soil structure, whether you have a heavy soil or a light one. It is an ideal long-term strategy to make it easier for plant roots to thrive.

You are disposing of waste material and using it *in situ*.

You know exactly what the ingredients are.

Wormery compost is beautifully fine and crumbly. See the compost recipes in 'Containers'.

If that lot doesn't convince you then what hope is there?

No-dig Growing

*The thin skin of a field ripped into shreds by the blunt scalpel of a plough.
Weeds and worms, fungi and fauna, all surf out of the dark on a curling wave
of ploughshare soil.*

Digging is the domestic ploughing, and when not trying to write bits of bad
prose, perhaps we should be out there wielding a spade.

But hold fast – for every reason given for digging, there is an alternative
solution: from relieving compaction (don't compact it in the first place) to
burying organic matter (apply it as a mulch).

It makes sense not to do it if it is not
necessary; it makes even more sense if
digging can have negative effects.

CORRECT WAY
TO HOLD A SPADE
(DIGGING SYSTEM)

Yes, apart from giving you a bad back,
digging and rotovating can do naughty
things. The soil's flora and fauna that help
plants grow can be killed by exposure to
light, drying out and chopping up – there will
be up to 20 times more worms in no-dig
compared to cultivated land – and the natural
soil structure is destroyed. This is ok in the
short term, since vegetables growing in it
will benefit from the extra air and release of
nutrients, resulting from digging. But the soil
slumps after a while and requires digging
again to re-introduce air. You are on a
treadmill of annual cultivation.

CORRECT WAY TO
HOLD A SPADE
(NO-DIG SYSTEM)

You may enjoy digging; it is certainly a form
of exercise, particularly if done with a good
technique: one that doesn't threaten your
back. It will produce good results as long as
it is done repeatedly.

However, if you can get as good results, if not better, with less work, time
expended and damage to the soil's inhabitants, then maybe it is worth trying a
different approach.

You can get good exercise (mental) by sitting in a deckchair watching other
people dig, maybe even cheering them on.

For no-dig growing to succeed, it has to mimic nature and in so doing protect the
soil structure and content. There is rarely any bare soil in nature – if there is, it
compacts with the weather and nutrients are lost through leaching. The soil

surface is always protected by either plants or plant matter. This is what we can do: at any one time the vegetable plot should be covered, preferably by crops or green manures (see 'Organic Growing Systems').

Other materials can be used to cover the soil, as mentioned in 'What to do first on a new plot', including black plastic, landscape fabric or cardboard. However, plants are nature's answer: when plants are growing they improve the structure, they protect against leaching and they reduce the effects of heavy rain on the soil surface.

A good covering of organic matter, like compost, can do much the same, even if it doesn't prevent leaching entirely. Furthermore, fine organic matter on the soil surface is perfect for sowing seeds into without having to generate a good 'tilth' in the soil.

There are a number of issues to do with no-dig growing that need to be resolved. What if there is already compaction of the soil? The remedy is deep forking, which can loosen airless soil; there is no need to lift it or turn it over, just push in the fork and pull backwards. Thereafter avoid compaction: no walking on the growing area and no bare soil.

How do we get rid of perennial weeds? Apart from using the black plastic/ cardboard method, they may have to be forked out, especially the deep-rooting ones, to the point when you might say: 'This is disturbance of the soil; this is digging, you fool'. Fair enough - there are no rules. So much for that.

Organic Growing Systems

A couple of different ways of growing organically are described below. You can follow either, neither, or a combination of both. Like all organic systems they would not involve chemicals of any kind. Both can be, or maybe should be, no-dig.

Compost Organic

Beds are prepared and well-rotted manure or compost is added to the surface. Seeds and plants are set out in this organic matter. After harvest, more compost is put on and the procedure is repeated. There is no rest for the land, but does there need to be?

Pros

Fertile soil

Soil develops a great structure

Few slugs (no hiding places)

Few weeds

Resilient crop plants

Cons

Leaching of nutrients when no crops are in, particularly on light soils.

Looks very neat but perhaps a bit boring?

Where does all of that compost come from?

A MIXTURE OF PLANTS ATTRACTS MORE WILDLIFE

The sluglessness only happens if the cropping area is quite large or you can control the plant growth and tidiness of the surrounding area. This is less likely in a back garden or on an allotment.

Plant Organic

Organic matter is added to the soil in a combination of home-made compost and green manures (plants grown specifically to maintain and improve the soil quality). The compost will often be applied as a mulch, put down around plants. The green manures will be sown after one crop has been harvested and will be killed off before the next goes in. This could be just a month or two, over winter, or as long as 18 months, if you have the space.

There would be lots of companion plants, flowers and other mixed plantings.

Pros

Beautiful

More sustainable – no, or reduced, inputs from outside.

Potentially less work than barrowing compost.

Little leaching occurs – plants occupy the land for most of the year.

More natural

Soil structure and depth improved by deep-rooting, green manures.

Cons

More weeds are likely (digging may be required to get them out)

More slugs

It is sometimes difficult to establish a green manure.

Killing off green manures can be tricky without digging; try hoeing with a very sharp hoe or chopping with an azada.

Notes on Green Manures

All green manures will improve soil structure through their roots and with the addition of organic matter. Some, like clover and tares will also add nitrogen to the soil. They are cut regularly and all matter is left on the soil surface, or dug in, but not removed.

Use the rapidly growing Phacelia and Buckwheat to fill in between crops. Use

ADDING ORGANIC MATTER TO BEDS......

... GREEN MANURES..   .... COMPOST

Tares, Field beans and, in milder areas of the country, Phacelia to cover the bare ground over winter. Try Red Clover for at least a year and-a-half as a rest for the soil, or 'ley'; this would constitute a whole block in a rotation whilst adding a wonderful amount of organic matter and nitrogen.

For further information on green manures see page 182.

Seeds, and Where to Find Them

Sowing seeds is such an endlessly fascinating activity. We carefully bury these tiny, 'dried' life-bombs year after year and still, when seedlings appear, it is as though it has happened for the first time. The carrots are up! Much running around and pointing at little, strap-like seed leaves ensues: 'Well, who would've thought it, etc.'

Maybe such joy is experienced because deep down we can't believe any such thing could actually happen. But it does – more often than not.

Maybe when I stop feeling like this each spring, it'll be time to hang me boots up.

The only time this doesn't happen – and this may only serve to reinforce the delight when germination does take place – is when I use old seed. I know they're old and I know I've not stored them well, yet I still sow them; 'shame to throw them away'. And then, nothing...

The correct way to store seeds is in a sealed container in the fridge, so that they are kept dry and cold; not in a desk drawer.

So, how long should we try to keep seed, because, let's face it, in most packets there are several years' worth of seeds?

Well, with good storage conditions, as described above, you should get three years out of any packet of seeds, with the possible exception of the maverick parsnip, which will only last one year. Thereafter, it depends on the vegetable. There are tables of longevity for vegetable seed giving you this information, but I suspect this is not valid if you have imperfect storage conditions. For example, it is said that large seeds will last a long time, however, my desk drawer peas keep very poorly, yet the small carrot and rocket seeds seem to go on and on.

A reasonable approach is to carry on using old seed until you see a noticeable change, like the time it takes to germinate compared to last time, or in comparison to new seed; the evenness of germination (have they all come up at once or sporadically) or have a number of seeds simply failed to appear at all? Seed merchants occasionally sell bad batches, and there have been complaints that a few retailers have consistently sold seed below the legal minimum-germination requirement.

To deal with this we usually sow at least two seeds where we want one plant, thinning out the weaker one in the process.

Anyway, if you notice any reduction in performance in old seed, get rid of it. It isn't going to get any better.

Seed Buying

A few questions about buying seeds:

Is it worth buying organic seeds instead of non-organic:

The answer is: Yes.

Next question, please.

Why?

Three answers ranked in ascending order of importance:

1. The seed will hold a small amount of chemicals from a plant raised in a non-organic system; a very small amount. Non-organic seed can have chemical dressings added.

2. The organic parent plant will have been raised in conditions similar to your organic patch and the offspring should be suitably adapted to organic growing conditions, we hope. (Sometimes the parent plants are raised in polytunnels or even abroad in quite different climates.)

3. By buying organic seed you are supporting organic growers.

So, which seed merchants should we buy from? Some are dedicated to trying to find organic sources, others just bolt on an organic selection to their 'mainstream' choice.

Try to find local suppliers. Contact, or even join, your local organic group and they may well have recommendations.

The Organic Gardening Catalogue sells non-organic, untreated seeds where it can't source organic seeds. As the name suggests, it is dedicated to organic growing. *www.organiccatalogue.com*

Tamar Organics is a small, modest but genuine company based in the South West that now sells only organic seeds. *www.tamarorganics.co.uk*

Tuckers Seeds is also based in the South West, with lots of hybrid seeds. *www.tuckers.co.uk*

Real Seeds is a great, small company in West Wales promoting seed saving and sells only open-pollinated seeds (no hybrids). They are not registered as organic, but many of their seeds come from organic growers. *www.realseeds.co.uk*

Jekka's Herb Farm (run by the dynamic Jekka McVicar) has a great range of organic herb seed, including some salads and vegetables. *www.jekkasherbfarm.com*

Vital Seeds and Ethical Organic Seeds are both new on the scene, very like Real Seeds but with organic certification. *www. vitalseeds.co.uk* and *www.ethicalorganicseeds.co.uk*

Secret Seeds has as strong an emphasis on flowers as well as vegetables, with some unusual varieties. *www.secretseeds.co.uk*

Duchy Originals offers a smallish range of purely organic seeds. *www.duchyoriginals.co.uk,* now sold via Thompson and Morgan.

Compare prices, like for like; the numbers of seeds in a packet varies enormously, so take note before purchasing.

What about those packets of really cheap seed from supermarkets?

Anything that is really cheap has a cost elsewhere. With seeds it is either with the grower making a loss or little money due to pressure from the retailer, or with you having poor quality, or even non-existent seedlings.

Seed Saving

Rather than buying seed on a regular basis, we can, with a little endeavour, save our own.

Think about this: if you select good plants on your plot and collect the seed from them (using the directions below) and do this on a regular basis, eventually you will still have the same variety you started with, but one that is adapted to your plot and your growing conditions. Brilliant.

Important: the first thing to note is that this can only be done with plants that are called open-pollinators or self-pollinators; not with hybrids.

Self-pollinators are plants that will produce seed just by themselves, without insects to transfer pollen between plants. In some cases, the flowers will have been pollinated and fertilised before the flowers have even opened. This has the charming name of 'cleistogamy' or 'hidden marriage'. How romantic.

The significance of this is that we can collect seed from self-pollinators, sow it and produce plants just like the parents. In other words, the variety (or to be more correct, 'cultivar') is maintained.

Unfortunately, there aren't many vegetables that do this. They are: lettuce, most tomatoes, peas and French beans, and for these it is excellent news, because after buying an initial packet of seed, we need never buy another. It is easy to collect the seed of these plants, with the exception of lettuce, one or two of which need to be left – obviously unharvested – until they have sent up a flower and set seed, all taking time and space.

Well, that's the easy ones out of the way; now for virtually every other vegetable.

Plants that are open-pollinators won't set seed unless pollen has been transferred between at least two different plants, and this is normally done by insects, especially bees. If we want to save seed of a particular variety, then the pollen being exchanged has to be between specimens of that same variety. It is no use having plants of different varieties crossing because you won't know what you will get – unless you are a plant breeder, when this is exactly what you want to do.

Your task is therefore to ensure only the correct pollen reaches a given flower. The easiest example is with squash, which unusually in the vegetable world, has separate male and female flowers on the same plant. The male flower produces pollen and sends it off to other plants via insects, whilst the female flower receives useful pollen from the male flowers of other plants. If we want to save seed from a particular variety, say 'Sweet Dumpling', then we protect the female flower from incoming insects (who knows where they've been?) and introduce pollen specifically from the male flower of a different plant of 'Sweet Dumpling'. Result? Seeds in the fruit produced from that flower will develop into only 'Sweet Dumpling' plants. How do we tell the difference between male and female flowers? The males have a straight stalk behind the yellow flower and the female has a small swelling, a mini fruit, immediately behind its flower. How do we keep insects off the female flower?

A fine mesh bag will do it, fitted before the flower opens.

AN OPEN MALE
FLOWER

A PARTIALLY OPEN
FEMALE FLOWER

How do we ensure pollination?

We remove a male flower from a different plant of the same variety when it's opened, take off its petals and – how can I say this delicately? – 'introduce' it to the female flower. Or you could use a dry paint brush to transfer pollen from male to female flowers. To be precise, pollen has to get on the end of the projecting structure in the female flower (the 'stigma'). You may, if you wish, make a buzzing noise as you do this. Remember to put back the bag after your pollinating: insects could still bring in the wrong pollen until the flowers have withered (when the bag can be removed and a label attached).

Other vegetables have different issues, but the principles are just the same. With many of them you can't leave the plant intact and harvest and eat it as we do with squash; we have to sacrifice the plant just to produce seed. This involves waiting until it flowers, which can be the following year.

For example: kale is left unpicked all winter; any poor plants, or those attacked by pests and diseases, are removed. The remaining plants should number at least twelve, preferably twenty, which is a lot of kale plants, but is necessary to ensure genetic diversity.

The flowers of kale are small and in clusters, and the male and female parts are contained in each flower. This doesn't matter; just exclude insects at flowering time (sheets of fleece are best) and do the dry paintbrush trick between all the plants. It is fiddly and time-consuming but will produce bags of seed eventually.

Get your friends to save a different vegetable each and you can exchange your seed harvest.

The seed we collect is in the 'fruit' (pods or heads) and will usually be left to dry almost to the point where the seeds start dropping. The fruit at this point should be in a paper bag so that as they finish drying, any seed that is shed is caught. Seed may need to be physically removed from the dried structure.

With some vegetables the fruit of which is eaten, like squash and tomatoes, the seeds are extracted from the pulp or fleshy fruit, then cleaned and dried.

There are some great additions to the 'dead easy' school of seed saving:

1. Where you not only don't need to worry about crossing with other varieties, but you may also be pleased to have it happen. This can be the case with flowers. Say if you had nasturtiums growing around your plot, you can simply collect the seed when it forms and next year's enjoy the range of flower colours. You could of course, simply let them drop and weed them out where you don't want them.

    If you wanted a particular colour of nasturtium flower, then it would be a different matter.

2. The other time we can relax is when there will be nothing to cross pollinate with our chosen plants. A great example would be New Zealand spinach. It is extremely unlikely that anything related to this will be growing nearby so simply collect the seed at the end of the season.

    Ta-dah.

Pests, Diseases and Preventions

Hopefully, your crops will always be pristine. In the event that a creature or pathogen has the temerity to have a go, this chapter is to reassure you that it is not always a disaster – frequently just a mild irritation – and there are ways of dealing with them.

The control of pests and diseases (P & D) is perhaps the most defining difference between organic and chemical growing.

I will not recommend any pesticide sprays in this book, whether organic or not. The few organic chemicals that are available, including homemade ones like rhubarb leaves, can have issues. Derris, an insecticide used for years in organic systems, has now been banned because of cancer-inducing properties. Even soft soap, which contains fatty acids, and is as benign a spray as you can get, will also dispatch beneficial insects like ladybirds.

There are some sprays that don't kill anything; just discourage P & D. For example, garlic blended with water and sprayed on leaves, will deter many pests.

Also, a tea made from horsetail (the plant, not the horse) will coat leaves with silicon and prevent the germination of fungal spores. Repeat applications are required for them to work.

Each pest or disease will have its

FLEECE LAID OVER CROPS
WOULD NORMALLY
LAST AT LEAST A SEASON

weak spot for you to exploit and, interestingly, trying to kill them should come pretty low down the list. Barriers (something to stop the P or D physically reaching your crops) are exceptionally useful. The most common barrier is fleece, which is a spun material in a sheet that is laid over the crop before the pest gets busy. It is weighed down around the edges (some folk dig it in but this creates maintenance problems). There are different grades: the thicker you buy the longer it will last: go for $25gm/m^2$. Even then, it is tricky getting more than one season's worth out of a sheet.

An alternative to fleece is a very fine mesh net found under names like Micromesh, Enviromesh, etc. This can last for many years but doesn't give as much frost protection as fleece. To keep out the smallest pests like flea beetle you'll need to get the ultrafine version. It is more expensive than fleece, but its added lifespan makes it extremely attractive.

Getting other things to do the work is even better than the use of barriers, if you can rely on them. This is something chemical growers rarely achieve, because they are on a killing treadmill which involves poisoning the pest whereby you also kill the predator of the pest at the same time, or starve it. A theme that is returned to a number of times in this little bookling is the one where we should try to imitate nature as much as possible. There are few pests or diseases that badly affect our native plants, except for introduced ones, of course. There are also rarely monocultures to be found in nature: grassland that hasn't been sprayed is full of non-grass plants; beech woodlands have much more than beech trees, with amazing sub-canopies and herbaceous layers.

So how can we replicate this in growing vegetables? The most direct answer is to stop growing annual vegetables and rely instead on permanent plantings. Here, we are strolling happily in the direction of permaculture and forest gardening. If you do nothing else with your life, investigate these two concepts; but not here. Besides, I'm quite partial to a carrot or two, addicted to baked potatoes and positively unhinged about curly kale, all of which require soil disturbance to some degree; and that is not a common feature of a forest garden.

The alternative is to grow a range of plants together: your chosen vegetable in smallish blocks with other plants amongst or alongside them. Unless you have a tiny growing area, then this should not involve breaking your rotation by mixing up all of your vegetables. Some people will advocate this, but it is a planning nightmare: trying to sort out how much of any one crop you are going to end up with.

Instead, introduce lesser cropping plants amongst your main crop (otherwise known as intercropping) like radishes with Brussels sprouts, lettuce with squash, etc. This is also a great way of using those gaps between widely-spaced slower-growing crops. Or use flowers. What? Flowers? This is a vegetable garden not an herbaceous border, which is to say...

Companion Planting

Companion planting is where one plant is grown close to another plant to benefit the growth of one or both of them. It can be vegetable and vegetable or vegetable and flower, and generally the mechanisms involved in most interactions are unclear. However, one thing is for certain: many flowers encourage predators of pests and are therefore invaluable. They also look rather splendid. For example, try planting:

Calendula (English or pot marigold) to attract lacewings.

Cosmos, fennel and related plants, or Limnanthes (poached egg plant) all to attract hoverflies;

Nettles (yes, plant nettles) to attract ladybirds.

The above insects will consume a range of pests but particularly aphids.

Other ways that companion plants can work are:

1. By repelling insect pests. For example,

Marigolds (*Tagetes* sp.) can repel nematodes (microscopic worms that can attack roots) with root exudates (amino acids & lactose) and repel whitefly with the smell of volatile oils (kolines) released from the leaves; onions can deter carrot root fly by masking the smell of carrots. This requires mixing the onion and carrot families in the rotation.

2. By attracting insect pests.

The idea here is that the companion plant draws the pest away from your crop. Arguments against make the point that pests are actually attracted to the area and maybe even helped in building up their numbers. e.g. Nasturtiums attract blackfly away from crop plants.

Nettles attract nettle aphid (that won't feed on your crops) early in the year and ladybirds move in after them. If you cut down the nettles, ladybirds will move on to crop plants.

3. By encouraging crop plants:

e.g. Marigolds (*Tagetes* sp.) planted with Tomatoes offer beneficial root exudates (see 'Allelopathy' p.180)

4. By discouraging weeds:

Tagetes minuta (or Mexican marigold) can be effective against ground elder, couch grass etc. Cut down Ground Elder with shears and plant 15cm (6ins) high specimens of *Tagetes* at 30cm (1ft) intervals for the best effect (see 'Allelopathy' p.180).

5. By creating mutually beneficial conditions:

Squash plants, under sweet corn, suppresses weeds, as well as keeping the ground moist and shaded, which sweet corn likes. Sometimes beans are included, fixing nitrogen and climbing the corn plants. This is known as 'the three sisters'. If you try it, use wider spacings than those given for the individual crops.

6. By accessing nutrients or making them available:

Nitrogen-fixing plants like peas and beans or clover, bring nitrogen from the atmosphere into the soil. Deep-rooting plants, such as alfalfa or chicory, bring up minerals. The nutrients from all of these plants can become available to your crops from their leaves when they die back; or you cut them down.

Not a companion plant, but still designed to bring in predators, is 'the beetle bank'. A ridge of soil raised up to 30cm (1ft) with tussocky grass growing on it will house many beetles, which like the drier conditions. There can be 1500 carabid or ground beetles per square metre and they all eat slugs, their eggs and aphids amongst others. Where you get the soil from is a problem; certainly don't take it off your growing area. Perhaps by simply having raised, no-dig beds with good coverage of plants will be enough.

The following list of pests and diseases is compiled from those found under each vegetable covered in this book. It is by no means comprehensive but should deal with the main problems you might encounter. Due to their ubiquitousness and great notoriety, slugs (and snails) have their own chapter.

Aphids, Including Blackfly and Grey Aphids

Appearance: Known collectively as aphids, or greenfly despite the range of colours, you will normally see blackfly before noticing their effect on the plant, which is reduced vigour. Other aphids, which are camouflaged better, are noticeable when plants are stunted; often yellowing with sticky leaf surfaces and little white flecks (aphid skins). The odd one out is the lettuce root aphid, which you don't see until the ailing plant is pulled up.

Remedy: Physical removal: by hand with a dry paintbrush or a jet of water. Plant flowers to attract predators, in anticipation of infestations.

Badgers

Appearance: Large, black and white hairy things. The visible damage is toppled sweet corn plants and chewed cobs.

Remedy: Since sweet corn is the main plant targeted by badgers, it may be worthwhile giving it a miss for a year or two. Few physical barriers will stop a badger from taking its chosen route. Commercially, battery-operated electric fences are used.

A LARGE PEST CAN CAUSE A LOT OF DAMAGE

Birds

Appearance: Most of those causing damage are pigeons, though other birds go for seeds, seedlings, and onion sets. The remnants of seedlings are left on the surface; onion sets are thrown around.

Remedy: Netting. Try to put it on a frame or propped up on canes with plastic bottles on the ends as a support. Check regularly to see they are not trapped. Also try scarers, e.g. old CDs, suspended from a line, which flash in the light as they turn in the breeze.

Blackfly

Appearance: Small, black, roundish, sucking insects along the leaf veins of beetroot and peas and beans and on the pods of the latter.

Remedy: See 'Aphids'.

Blight, late

Appearance: In a wet year, brown and yellow patches may appear on the leaves of potatoes and tomatoes, usually in August though it can be as early as July. Leaves and stems die, and potato tubers eventually rot.

Remedy: Use blight-resistant varieties. Grow early varieties of potato; keep the leaves dry and ventilated (easiest with tomatoes and container-grown potatoes); remove foliage at first signs of infection to stop it reaching the potato tubers, or with tomato plants, to reduce its spread.

Blossom End Rot

Appearance: The bottom of a tomato fruit is sunken and black or brown.
Remedy: This is a disorder rather than disease, caused by lack of calcium, usually made worse by erratic watering. Water evenly.

Cabbage Root Fly

Appearance: Brassicas lack vigour, or even collapse. When the plants are pulled, maggots may be seen in the roots.

Remedy: Make a little cardboard collar to fit around the stem of each plant, in contact with the ground, and so stop the fly laying eggs next to the stem. This is worthwhile when you have fewer, big plants like broccoli, sprouts and kale. For any brassicas, use fleece or very fine mesh.

A CARDBOARD CABBAGE-ROOT-FLY COLLAR.

Cabbage White Butterfly

Appearance: The small CWB caterpillar (larva) is green, velvety and hides in the middle of brassicas, whereas the large CWB larva is hairy, black and yellow, and bigger. Damage is often seen first in holes, mostly within the leaf, as opposed to around the edge.
Remedy: Removal by hand; use *Bacillus thuringiensis* biological control spray; small mesh netting.

Carrot Root Fly

Appearance: Poor top growth, maybe some pink or yellow leaves; rusty, brown tunnels around the roots.
Remedy: Fleece or very fine mesh netting. See 'Carrots'.

Celery Fly/Celery Leaf Miner

Appearance: Leaves have dried up patches on them caused by grubs tunnelling within. Serious infestations give plants a scorched appearance and celery stalks are thin and unpleasant.
Remedy: Pick off marked leaves as soon as seen. If severe attacks are noted in successive years, cover with fleece after planting out.

Chocolate Spot

Appearance: Brown spots appear on the upper surface of the leaves of broad beans, and later on the pods. Yield is reduced.
Remedy: Improve drainage before sowing and ensure good ventilation and wider spacing.

Clubroot

Appearance: Stunted, coloured foliage, collapsing plants in dry weather and knobbly, distorted roots. It is a fungus-like organism in the soil.

Remedy: Lime the soil before planting. Grow broccoli, kale, sprouts etc to as big a size as possible before planting out. Some resistant varieties are available. As long a rotation as possible.

Cucumber Mosaic Virus

Appearance: Stunted plants show a mosaic pattern of yellow on the leaves. Any fruit is small, blotched and inedible.

Remedy: Use resistant varieties. Aphids spread the virus and weeds can harbour it, so control of both will help. Infected plants should be removed immediately.

Downy Mildew

Appearance: Many plants can suffer from downy mildew, though it won't spread between different types of vegetable. A yellow patch on the leaves' upper surfaces will have a corresponding greyish-white growth underneath.

Remedy: Avoid wet conditions if possible; good ventilation; wider spacing; no overhead watering. Remove infected leaves promptly.

Flea Beetle

Appearance: Many tiny holes in the leaves of brassicas. Small, shiny, often striped beetles jump off when the leaves are touched; worse in hot, dry conditions on young plants.

Remedy: Keep well-watered. Fleece should be fitted straight after sowing particularly in the spring/early summer.

Frit Fly

Appearance: The leaves of sweet corn have pale yellow stripes and then become frayed. Little white grubs may be found at the bases of the leaves.

Remedy: Not a common problem, but if your plot has a history of it use fleece on the young plants for the first couple of months. This protects the plants and gets them to a good size and strength in case they are attacked later.

Fusarium Wilt

Appearance: This fungus enters roots and blocks the transport system of the plant. The top of the plant dies.

Remedy: Remove affected plants promptly. Use a long rotation period.

Grey Aphids

Appearance: A fatter, mealy, grey aphid found on brassicas.

Remedy: See aphids.

Grey Mould

Appearance: A fluffy, cuddly, grey fungal growth, a.k.a. Botrytis. Found on fruit, including beans.

WHAT CAUSED THE DAMAGE
TO MY BRASSICAS?

PIGEONS – JAGGED EDGE
– LEAF RIBS LEFT
BEHIND

CABBAGE WHITE BUTTERFLY
CATERPILLARS – HOLES,
MAINLY IN THE MIDDLE

SLUGS/SNAILS – HOLES
(AND SLIME TRAILS) –
MIDDLE & EDGE

Remedy: Pick off when seen. Maintain good air flow; perhaps use wider spacing if occurring regularly.

Halo Blight
Appearance: French and runner bean leaves can develop small, angular spots, each one surrounded by a bright yellow ring. The leaves become completely yellow and die, affecting yields.
Remedy: Pick off affected leaves; try to keep the leaves dry and don't save seeds from diseased plants.

Leek Moth
Appearance: Small holes and marks on the foliage. The moth, tunnelling into the shaft of the leek, can allow in rots, and the plants collapse.
Remedy: Cut the top off the leek. If a tunnel is still visible on the cut surface, remove some more. Keep going until it is clear. The stump will re-grow. Or just use fleece straight after planting.

Mildew
Appearance: Leaves powdery (white on top) and downy (white underneath). Mildews are easily confused.
Remedy: Study the two types, that are described here separately.

Mice
Appearance: Cute, though I don't know if you've noticed that their feet are always cold.
Remedy: Dust peas with chilli powder and sow more deeply. Harvest sweet corn promptly. Release mice from humane traps over ½ mile away.

Onion Eelworm / Stem and Bulb Eelworm
Appearance: Tiny unsegmented worms, also known as nematodes, infest onion plants which are distorted and puckered ('onion bloat').
Remedy: A little is tolerable on a plant but may make it rot in store. Obviously affected onions should be taken off site. Use a long rotation (and clean sets).

Onion Fly

Appearance: Larvae of the fly tunnel into bulbs and the main problem is rots, which follow. Young plants can collapse and die.

Remedy: Fleece or fine mesh should be used from spring onwards. Infested plants (complete with maggots) should be removed carefully and taken off site.

Parsnip Canker

Appearance: Orange or black markings around the root, especially near the top. Other rots may enter.

Remedy: Rotation. Resistant varieties.

Pea and Bean Weevil

Appearance: Semi-circular notches are noticeable around the edges of leaves of peas and broad beans. Occasionally a small, grey beetle-thing will be found hiding amongst the new leaves.

Remedy: Nothing too much to worry about, though the growth of young plants can be checked. Use fleece on young plants.

Pea Moth

Appearance: Grubs and frass (insect excrement) are found inside pods of peas.

Remedy: Tolerate it (in other words, be selective when podding peas) or put fleece over plants just before flowering starts – not easy when they are on twigs or sticks for support. Sow early crops, avoid maincrops.

Pigeons

Appearance: Large, fat greedy thing with small head and large beak. Damage is often severe and is mainly found on leafy brassicas, with often just the ribs of leaves left, with pecking around the edge.

Remedy: Raised netting. Scarers such as dangling CD's or pictures of Boris Johnson.

Potato Cyst Eelworm

Appearance: Microscopic, unsegmented worm. Golden or brown spherical cysts attached to potato roots or rhizomes. Usually, any sign of attack is a failed plant or stunted growth.

Remedy: A long rotation. See 'Potatoes, Maincrop' for more exciting information.

Powdery Mildew

Appearance: White powdery fungal growth, appearing on the upper surface of leaves.

Remedy: This is worse when the soil is dry, yet the atmosphere is humid; also when plants are near the end of their lives. Remove infected leaves; keep well watered; use resistant varieties and/or preventative sprays.

Root Rots

Appearance: Soil-borne diseases infect roots or enter where there is other damage.

Remedy: Use a rotation and avoid physical damage to the plant.

Rust

Appearance: Orange or brown dots; yellowing leaves. A fungus.

Remedy: Remove infected leaves as soon as seen and take off site. Use a wider spacing initially.

Slugs and Snails

Appearance: Generally unattractive.

Remedy: See next page.

Soil-Borne Diseases

Appearance: A very wide, fairly useless category, encompassing a range of (mainly) fungi that attack roots and is noticed only when the top growth collapses.

Remedy: Rotation of at least four years, preferably eight.

Stem Eelworm

Appearance: Eelworms or nematodes are microscopic worms that attack plants or other soil creatures. Onion eelworm will make young plants distorted, stunted and useless. Older onion plants that become infected will produce bulbs that rot in store.

Remedy: Use good quality sets; rotations; remove and take infested plants off site.

Verticillium Wilt

Appearance: Discolouration may be seen between leaf veins (brown or yellow); plant tops may wilt and die. The transport system is discoloured with brown or black streaks and blocked by this fungus.

Remedy: Remove plants promptly. Practice hygiene to prevent passing it between plants.

White Rot

Appearance: A soil-borne disease. Onions and garlic leaves go yellow and collapse. White, fluffy, cotton wool-like growth on the base of the bulb, which just lifts out of the ground.

Remedy: Take affected plants off site immediately. Use a long rotation. Start off garlic in pots and use onion sets to get a head start.

Slugs and Snails

Apparently, there are 23 species of slugs in the UK. I think I've got them all on my plot.

Most are detritivores – they eat dead matter; in fact, they clean it up. Good for you, slugs, eh? Who would have thought it?

Anyway, the few that are a problem, make up for their uniqueness by appearing in huge numbers in a wet summer. Interestingly, a wet spring is probably worse – just when we are trying to establish tiny seedlings and transplants, which are vulnerable to even small slugs.

The old joke of 'What is a slug? – A snail with a housing problem' would be almost amusing if it were true. But slugs know where to go. Many, like the field slug and garden slug (both of them little ones), are soil dwellers. In dry weather, their home could be several feet down. The big black slug (or orange rimmed brown version) needs hiding places like weeds, long grass, leaves close to the ground, etc. Snails also like hiding places and will dominate in back gardens where the lime mortar of old walls provides them with shell-building material.

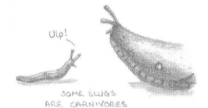

SOME SLUGS
ARE CARNIVORES

On a field scale, it is the small slugs that dominate, simply because there are fewer hiding places for the larger ones and for snails. That may be first choice for those of us with gardens or allotments: a good tidy-up. See 'Organic Growing Systems'.

Let us assume that we haven't managed to keep our plots pristine, and that we have a healthy population of slugs and snails of all sizes. Here are a few strategies; try a number of them together:

Cultural

Apart from trying to keep weeds down and cutting the grass around the edges regularly, light hoeing (which is supposed to disturb molluscs' trails) and keeping the soil dry, can help enormously. For the latter bit, you can go against the grain and water in the morning. By the evening the soil surface has dried; result – 80% less damage, apparently. The main drawback is, of course, rain.

Barriers

Forget the various grits and powders, such as ground eggshells, to sprinkle in rings around your plants. They may work for a while, but the slug eventually just says: 'Well, my underneath isn't going to enjoy trundling over this mildly unpleasant scratchy stuff, but I'm starving', and then scoffs the lot. Complete exclusion works – the bottom half of clear plastic bottles pushed into the ground over plants.

Water also works: a vegetable bed with a moat around it – horribly fiddly – or the seedlings on a table with its legs in dishes of water.

Fleece or fine mesh works well if you can bury the edges and ensure no slugs are trapped inside.

Something that does work on containers is a double band (about half-an-inch apart) of self-adhesive copper tape near the top. Apparently, it gives the slug a mild electric shock; but not cheap.

Traps

The idea here is that you encourage slugs to accumulate in a place of your choice. Whether it is a little piece of black plastic, half a grapefruit skin or a sacrificial lettuce, you still have to deal with the rotters when you catch them. The gentlest and possibly least effective destination, could be the compost heap where, theoretically, they should be happy as Larry. I wonder who Larry was and whether he'd be very chuffed to be deposited in a compost heap. Traps are most effective when checked – and cleared – regularly.

At least with beer traps they kill themselves: you need to get hold of the right beer (stout, heavy ale) – try homebrew or pub slops. They can capture quite a few, in alcoholic bliss, though the beer has to be renewed every few days.

Products

Ferric phosphate is a kind of blue pellet; not to be confused with Metaldehyde, a poison that will kill animals and birds, as well as slugs. It is allowed in organic systems because it breaks down to plant nutrients and 'affects no other organisms' – if used correctly. It's probably at its most effective in the spring when used on the breeding population and the young of the big black slug. Can be quite expensive.

More expensive still, but quite effective in a closed area like a back garden or greenhouse, are naturally-occurring microscopic worms called nematodes or eelworms that sneak up on the slug, invade it, feed, reproduce and terminate the host and … Sorry, I'm feeling a little queasy now.

STOP PRESS – Cats

Cats are beautiful, furry, cuddly and thoroughly lovable puddy tats, but... for gardeners they can be a downright nuisance. To put it bluntly: a pest, i.e. frog-torturing, sparrow-crunching, selfish despoilers of seed beds.

Remedies (excluding unwarranted illegal measures): water pistol (effective but you need to be quick on the draw); high-pitched electronic devices (work well on cats with non-impaired hearing, though pricey); cover bare soil – nets, sticks, thorny things (prevent unwelcome toilet habits, but fiddly); pepper, chilli powder (amusing to observe, but needs regular renewing).

Growing in Containers

For those of you who do not have a garden or allotment but want to dip your toe, tentatively, in the horticultural water, growing in containers is an attractive option. Who knows, perhaps it will lead to bigger and better things, in time? For a discussion on the pros and cons of growing in containers, see page 150

Step-by-step Procedure

Obtain a container – a good start. One of the fun things about all of this is you can use a huge range of receptacles, from old cans to tyres, tin baths to footwear. I tried growing plants in my old boots once – nothing seemed to survive. Can't understand why.

Make sure that the containers are the right size for the vegetables to be grown. There have been records of gardeners growing tomatoes in baked bean cans; admittedly to get just one truss of fruit. However, this can really stress the plants and they need a lot more looking after, including watering several times a day. Whatever you use, it is important to clean it thoroughly, especially if it contained contaminants. It is often recommended that you sterilise them. You can buy products for the purpose, though some are pretty

MANY DIFFERENT CONTAINERS CAN BE USED TO GROW VEGETABLES

unpleasant. Try a brand of lemon-based disinfectant found in organic catalogues, which also helps keep rainwater butts clean. If your container has previously held strong, healthy plants, it is now believed that you don't need to clean them. In fact, the compost still stuck to the sides can contain beneficial micro-organisms. It's a different matter if you suspect those plants were diseased…..

Next ensure that there is adequate drainage. By that, it is meant there should be holes in the bottom. If there are only a few, or they are very small, then add a good (2.5cm (1in)) layer of grit and/or put pieces of crock arching over each hole. Another name for crock is pieces from that old clay flower pot you dropped a few weeks ago.

A couple of examples: an old sink is great, especially those big white ceramic jobs that you once saw on Coronation Street. It looks good, it's heavy – meaning that it is stable – and it will usually be of a reasonable volume, leaving space for roots. However, it has only one exit for water draining out, namely the plug hole.

Place a piece of crock or bit of tile over the hole and add a layer of grit, so that water percolating downwards can eventually move sideways to the hole.

An old olive oil tin would need holes punched in the bottom, usually using a hammer and a large nail. You can make lots of holes like this, but they will be fairly small and will project inwards, so a layer of grit or small stones is important to stop the compost blocking them.

Stand your container on a few pebbles so that it doesn't seal to the ground or make a few holes in the side of the container, near the bottom if possible.

Find some, potting compost, or more correctly, growing medium to fill your containers. This would be peat-free and organic-based (as opposed to soil-based, which is heavier and more suited to long-term plantings in containers). There are many brands, all with varying degrees of reliability. This is your chance to experiment. The biggest issue is probably how well it will keep your vegetables going – in other words, how much fertility it has and can retain, and the ability to keep a steady supply of water available.

For the more adventurous amongst you, you can try making your own, without buying-in ingredients. Here are a couple of recipes for growing media (ingredients by volume):

a) 1 part worm compost (This is from a wormery, but could be well-formed garden compost).
   3 parts leaf mould
b) 1 part garden compost (This recipe includes soil, making it heavier).
   1 part loam
   1 part leaf mould

All ingredients would need to be sieved and the loam (a decent garden soil) has to be pasteurised (not sterilised). You can place a tray of soil in the oven, covered with foil, and leave at 80°C for 30 minutes.

HE, HE, HE !
TWO PARTS LEAF MOULD , ONE PART WORM COMPOST...

An interesting question is: where do you get the plants from? Usually, the answer would be 'from a packet of seeds', but it may not be a good idea to sow directly into your container; one that is filled with a strong compost, designed for a season's sustained growth.

A few options:

Buy them: extra cost, unfortunately, plus have they been organically grown and are they carrying a pest or disease?

You can grow them yourself indoors, using seed compost in trays or modules and in a pleasant, warm, light environment until they have at least two true leaves. The difficulty here is getting the right conditions, i.e. the warm, light environment (see 'Sowing Seeds'). Remember to harden them off before transplanting out into the containers. This involves getting them used to being outside by putting them out during the day and taking them back in for the night. Some vegetables, like carrots, won't transplant well, so they have to be sown directly. Add a weaker, seed compost to the potting compost, as a top layer, and sow into that. A transition layer (a mixture of both composts) could be created between the seed compost and the potting compost, if you're feeling a bit ambitious.

Watering is clearly a key feature of growing in containers. How much you have to do depends on a number of things, like the type of compost, the vegetable and its stage of growth, and the weather. If pots need plunging in a bucket of water to re-wet them, then you've miscalculated, but then you probably knew that. Ideally, the compost should stay evenly moist, and when watering, a small amount should emerge from the bottom of the container.

CONTAINERS REQUIRE CAREFUL, EVEN WATERING

You can reduce how much you need to water considerably by having your containers in sheltered positions. The less exposure to wind and hot sun, the less evaporation will take place.

Feeding requirements are also very variable. Hopefully, the compost would sustain the crop throughout its life, though if the size of the container limits the volume of compost too much you will have to help the plants, usually with a liquid feed. (See 'Fertility').

Occasionally, especially with a long-term crop, it may be wise to add a top dressing around the growing plants. This could be more potting compost, so acting as a mulch, as well as providing some nutrients; or as a dry, organic fertiliser sprinkled on, then gently forked into the surface of the compost.

What do you do with the compost at the end of the crop? Lettuce and salads can be grown in spent compost, but it is not suitable for another crop which has high demands, like tomatoes. After the salads, the compost can go straight onto the garden – if you have one, that is.

Vegetables suitable for containers

- Most salads have low maintenance requirements and it is immensely satisfying to pop out of the back door to cut a few leaves just as you want them. Herbs such as basil, parsley and coriander would be similarly appreciated. Keep them as near to the kitchen as possible.

- Plants which tolerate being containerised, like tomatoes and, surprisingly, potatoes are fine.
- Plants which grow quickly and are eaten young, like radishes, short carrots, small beetroot and spinach are perfect.
- Plants which are problematic to grow out in the open, may do better in containers. Peppers and even possibly aubergines can produce a crop when grown in pots placed in sunny, sheltered places.

Vegetables that aren't suitable are ones that will need to be in the container for months and require an extensive root run. Can you grow parsnips in a pot? Yes, but badly; and why would you want to anyway? Courgettes in a container? Yes, but it needs to be of a good size. Sweet corn in a sink? Big sink.

Long term crops like winter brassicas and leeks don't do well.

Peas and beans summarise the approach. Dwarf peas and dwarf French beans work best of all; climbers including runner beans demand too much from the compost and require too much watering. There is a dwarf runner bean, 'Hestia', that is recommended for pots.

Sun or Shade?

Most vegetables do well with lots of sun. Some can tolerate a certain amount of shade, though probably at a cost to the yield, quality and maybe flavour. Still, it allows us to use places which would be otherwise unoccupied and still get something. Plus, you won't have to water so much....

The following list is, of course, transferable to the plot and doesn't just refer to containers, though on the plot you have a maggot-in-the-carrot with something called 'a rotation'. In other words, if you have a shady area, at some point every crop will have to be there. Not so with containers.

Here are a few vegetables reputed to be tolerant of some shade:

Beetroot, Calabrese, Kale, Kohlrabi, Lettuce, Radish, Spinach and the herbs Chives, Mint and Parsley.

Sowing and Planting Calendar

Exact timings for planting will vary depending on the area of the country. Those given are for mid-England and Wales. Adapt times for your location. Since this book refers to outdoor vegetables, the section 'Sowing Indoors', refers to the propagation stage; the resulting seedlings would be planted outside a month or two later (see '*Plant*' below).

An alternative to sowing indoors is sowing in a nursery seedbed – a little area outside used purely for raising plants before transplanting them elsewhere, e.g. leeks. The timing for sowing in a nursery seedbed is given in 'Sowing Indoors'. Some sowing/planting times are better than others for particular vegetables. For example, garlic can be planted any time between October and February, though the favoured month for many growers is November (check details in 'A-Z of Vegetables' if you are unsure).

January

Sow indoors: summer cauliflower.

Plant: garlic cloves.

February

Sow indoors: summer cabbage, kohl rabi, pea.

Plant: garlic cloves, lettuce.

March

Sow indoors: Brussels sprout, summer cabbage, calabrese, autumn cauliflower, celeriac, lettuce.

Sow direct outdoors: broad bean, beetroot, carrot, chard, kohl rabi, onion seed, parsnip, pea, radish, rocket, spinach, turnip.

Plant: asparagus, summer cauliflower, lettuce, horseradish, onion sets, potato tubers (early).

April

Sow indoors: asparagus pea, aubergine, French bean, runner bean, Brussels sprout, calabrese, autumn cauliflower, celery, courgette, cucamelon, cucumber, fennel, goosefoot, leek, lettuce, pepper, physalis, soya bean, squash, sweet corn, tomato.

Sow direct outdoors: beetroot, carrot, chard, kohl rabi, parsnip, pea, radish, rocket, spinach, swede, turnip.

Plant: asparagus, artichoke, summer cabbage, calabrese, autumn cauliflower, kohl rabi, lettuce, onion sets, pea, potato tubers (main).

May (late May*)

Sow indoors: French bean, purple-sprouting broccoli, winter cabbage, calabrese, callaloo, spring and autumn cauliflower, chicory, fennel, kale, lettuce, physalis, squash.

Sow direct outdoors: asparagus pea, runner bean*, beetroot, callaloo*, carrot, fennel, kohl rabi, lettuce, New Zealand spinach, parsnip, pea, radish, rocket, soya bean*, spinach, swede, turnip.

Plant: asparagus pea*, French bean*, runner bean*, Brussels sprout, summer cabbage, calabrese, autumn cauliflower, celeriac, celery, courgette*, cucamelon*, cucumber*, fennel, goosefoot*, lettuce, oca*, pepper*, physalis*, soya bean*, squash*, sweet corn*, sweet potato*, tomato*.

June

Sow indoors: spring cauliflower, chicory, fennel.

Sow direct outdoors: French bean, beetroot, calabrese, carrot, fennel, kohl rabi, lettuce, pea, radish, ramsons, rocket, spinach, swede, sweet corn, turnip.

Plant: aubergine, French bean, purple-sprouting broccoli, Brussels sprout, winter cabbage, calabrese, callaloo, spring and autumn cauliflower, celery, chicory, courgette, cucumber, fennel, goosefoot, leek, lettuce, pepper, physalis, squash, sweet corn, tomato.

July

Sow indoors: spring cabbage, fennel.

Sow direct outdoors: French bean, spring cabbage, chard, kohl rabi, lettuce, pea, radish, ramsons, rocket, spinach, turnip.

Plant: purple-sprouting broccoli, winter cabbage, calabrese, spring cauliflower, fennel, kale, leek, lettuce.

August

Sow indoors: spring cabbage.

Sow direct outdoors: spring cabbage, chard, corn salad, kohl rabi, lettuce, onion seed, radish, rocket, spinach, turnip.

Plant: chicory, fennel.

September

Sow indoors: kohl rabi, lettuce.

Sow direct outdoors: corn salad, radish.

Plant: spring cabbage.

October

Sow indoors: summer cauliflower, lettuce.

Sow direct outdoors: broad bean, pea.

Plant: spring cabbage, garlic cloves, kohl rabi, lettuce, onion sets.

November

Sow direct outdoors: broad bean, pea.

Plant: garlic cloves, lettuce.

December

Plant: garlic cloves.

Cloches

Sometimes it is just not enough to rely on the weather for vegetable growing: the answer is in your hands.

You can raise the temperature and protect your plants from the elements (and some pests) by putting up some temporary housing. This is commonly called a cloche and will warm plants and soil at either end of the summer. As a result, you can grow some vegetables for longer in the year, as well as cater for those which are slightly fussy: tomatoes spring to mind. You can even grow crops that are more at home outside the summer months that still need protection over winter; spinach, rocket, lettuce and other salads will thank you heartily for sticking a cloche over them.

Why, you might ask, are cloches called cloches. Good question. It is simply French for 'bell', and the link between that and a sheet of polythene suspended over your tomatoes is obvious, isn't it?

The original cloches were bell-shaped glass domes of various sizes, to fit over individual plants. You can still buy these (rather pricey), though if you want an economical version try cut-down plastic bottles.

The most common cloche, amusingly alluded to above, is a sheet of polythene (possibly fleece, netting or Environmesh) held above a crop on hoops. Any polythene can be used, but special 'UV-stabilised' sheets can be bought from garden centres, catalogues, etc., and will last a lot longer than that wrapper that used to be around your new sofa or mattress.

Commercially, the hoops would be sturdy wire bent into a semi-circle and pushed into the ground. The width of the polythene sheet matches the length of the semi-circle so that it reaches the soil either side.

To stop the polythene disappearing at the first breath of wind and wrapping itself intricately around your neighbour's apple tree, string is tied to the hoops at ground level having passed *over* the polythene.

The ends of these cloches are bunched together and weighed down with bricks or tied around a stake.

Wire hoops are normally bought ready made. Blue (or black) water pipe is a great alternative, mainly because you can make cloches big enough to span a bed. Water pipe is best slotted onto pegs of some description (bamboo/dowelling/metal pipe?) and the string will tie onto these pegs.

If the bed is 1.2m (4ft) wide it will take you no time at all to work out that your hoops and width of polythene need to be…hang on a bit…any second now… π x the radius of the semi-circular hoop = $^{22}/_7$ x 60cm (2ft) = about 190cm (or just over 6ft). Phew.

Hoops are spaced evenly along the bed, 60 to 90cm (2 to 3ft) between each one; closer spacings are stronger but fiddlier. Remember to leave gaps at the ends to hold down the polythene.

As for all-important watering, guess what? Just gently lift the side – the hoops will stay in place – and pour it in. The polythene stays up, which is not unhelpful when you might want a bit of ventilation too.

Having hoops-and-polythene cloches will look pretty professional and make

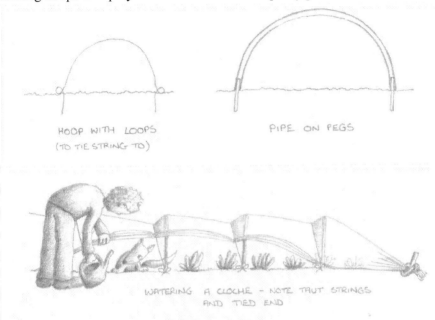

HOOP WITH LOOPS
(TO TIE STRING TO)

PIPE ON PEGS

WATERING A CLOCHE – NOTE TAUT STRINGS
AND TIED END

you the envy of all clocheless neighbours. However, any reliable structure you can concoct, made of timber, polythene, baler twine, chewing gum – anything that will protect and warm your plants – is worthwhile.

Other Related Matters
If you want to keep life simple, don't read this

This section includes bits that are either a little controversial, more complicated, or I couldn't think where else to put them.

Fertility, and awkward issues

Chemical-based industrial growers have a whole armoury of feeding methods at their disposal, calculating the exact amounts to apply and the financial, profit/loss perspective. Over the past six decades or so the fertilisers that have been used have concentrated on just the few nutrients that have the greatest effect on yields: nitrogen, phosphorus and potassium. This has resulted, over the years, in food low in vitamins and particular essential minerals, and in the creation of 'unbalanced' soils.

Comparisons between chemical and organic food nutritional levels have been a subject of controversy: it is very difficult to compare two systems that vary wildly within themselves. For example, there will be a difference between carrots produced on a long-established organic farm (if the soil there has been well looked after) compared to a newly converted organic farm running for a couple of years, on land that was previously used chemically. The same applies with non-organic farms.

It is often said that there is no difference between organic and non-organic sources of fertility, since the nutrients actually enter plant roots in the same form, no matter what the source. Unfortunately, this misses the point completely. Organic matter in particular, apart from often providing a complete range of nutrients, supplies and encourages beneficial soil organisms: quick-release chemical fertilisers dissolve rapidly and actually kill the nearby micro flora and fauna. The interaction of plants with micro-organisms in particular, is a huge area for research but could have effects as wide-ranging as protection from diseases and the ability of a plant to take up nutrients, to the flavour of the produce.

Containers, and, if we can get away with it, not using them

From one angle, growing anything in containers is bad news. The main issue is that they require compost to fill them.

The correct term is growing medium because 'compost' is confused with the stuff from that neglected heap in the corner of the garden. Growing media come from the garden centre in bags.

So, what's wrong with it?

Firstly, the cost, which may or may not be an issue.

Secondly, its origin: does it contain peat? There are people continually arguing about this, but without getting hung up on the issues, don't use it. Suffice it to say that the removal of peat from the environment has a disastrous effect on wildlife habitats. It is a carbon sink. Reliable, peat-free growing media are still being developed and most will be fine for growing vegetables. It's trickier, however, getting one suitable for raising seedlings.

Thirdly, the maintenance: There are two ways of looking at this. One is the joy that pottering about in your slippers and dressing gown in the morning, watering can in hand, can bring. The other is the extra work involved, and how easily it can go wrong. Keeping the moisture levels just right is an art in itself, especially when nature joins in just when she feels like it. Still, using good-sized containers, the right plants and fresh compost will make it easier.

From another angle, containers may be your only way of growing anything. How would we do without houseplants? What about the balcony of the flat on the third floor? What about those 'essential' plants that won't tolerate garden soil? What would we do with all those empty pots?

The answer may be somewhere in between. If you can do without containers, it will make life easier for you: lift some of those slabs in the patio; get rid of that car park in the front garden.

But if there is no alternative, then do it. Growing plants anywhere you can, has a lot going for it and is infinitely better than having none at all. Plants, including vegetables, can look terrific in pots and add another dimension to a domestic space. They are immense fun too, often being easier to plant up.

And one more major positive feature of containers: the plants are easier to protect from slugs.

Watering, rain versus tap

Collecting rainwater should be as fundamental as making a compost heap. Rainwater is, of course, the best irrigation water to use in all situations. The main problems arise when it has been stored, because pathogens can build up to such an extent that it is recommended that stored rainwater only be used on crops in open ground. We can minimise the issues by ensuring there is a lid on the butt and that in the autumn we empty and scrub it out. To keep the rainwater fresh try using soluble cleaner that is suitable for organic use and is added to the contents of the butt.

Some people advocate keeping goldfish in a water butt to keep it clean. This is a trifle unfair, particularly if you use a lid and if you extract water by dunking the watering can in the butt rather than taking it from the tap. You might find that you have fish and chips in the making when watering your spuds.

That leaves small containers and newly-sown trays etc. Use tap water that has been left to stand inside overnight in your watering can. It will warm up a little and allow the chlorine to evaporate, yet be free of pathogens.

Allelopathy, and what plants do to each other

One plant can affect another plant by way of the chemicals that it releases. This is the basis for many of the different combinations of plants used in 'companion planting'.

This can be positive or negative in effect – usually the latter – and it is to this that allelopathy usually refers.

Most plants have allelopathic interactions with each other, though the effect may be masked by greater interactions, like competition. The chemicals may be released in a variety of ways. They may be:

SOME PLANTS HAVE
WAYS OF KEEPING
OTHERS AT BAY

1. Washed from the leaves onto surrounding soil or plants.
2. Exuded from the roots (e.g. *Tagetes*).
3. Released from decomposing plant debris (certain green manures prevent seed germination after they have been dug in).
4. Released as volatile chemicals into the air from living leaves (aromatic herbs inhibit the growth of annual plants nearby, (combined with item 2)). Brassicas are believed to suppress weeds through both 2) and 3)), whilst barley inhibits the growth of chickweed and shepherd's purse.

Apart from crop plants, notable examples of allelopathy include grasses that, in addition to competition, inhibit the growth of trees, so slowing down the regeneration of woodland and its potential shading of the grasses. Similarly, heathers can prevent the establishment of birch and spruce by inhibiting mycorrhizal formation.

A positive example of allelopathy is Corncockle which increases the yield and quality of wheat.

There is an argument to be made that positive allelopathy is an accident: two plants which don't normally exist side by side, brought together and the chemical passed out by one happens to help the other. Negative allelopathy sounds more natural: one plant sends out a discouraging chemical signal to stop another plant from setting up shop right next door and taking the water and nutrients.

Much of the work done to establish which plants co-exist well with each other was done many years ago and could perhaps do with an update….

The Hungry Gap, and Perennial Plants

There will come a time when you might say that this vegetable-growing lark is all very well but there is still a time of year when you're reduced to raiding the freezer.

This is known as the hungry gap. If you haven't had a good year this could last from about January to perhaps December. Normally, it refers to late spring. By then the stored vegetables are past their best – if there are any left: potatoes emerge from the sack with the texture of a squash ball and sporting leg-like hairy, white shoots – large anaemic spiders. Onions have baggy bodies and long green shoots. Plants still in the ground from the previous year have developed attractive floral displays and almost useless edible parts – wooden parsnips, anyone? We'll eventually get tired of the work involved to extract any usable bits from these, not to mention the less than perfect textures and flavours; there is the whittling of carrots, the de-coring of parsnips, the searching for miniature flower buds on purple sprouting broccoli and the substituting of onion shoots for spring onions.

Anticipation may be the answer - once you've decided you've had enough of surgery on old vegetables it may be too late to do anything about the hungry gap – so plan ahead. This can be as long ago as the previous autumn with the planting of some overwintering crops like broad beans, spring cabbage and onions or it can be the sowing of some quick-growing plants for leaves or roots earlier that spring. For such leaves, try turnip tops (Namenia), komatsuna, texel greens or spinach. All are spinach-like, especially the last one, and can be used in salads or lightly cooked. The first three are in the cabbage family. For roots, try radish and early, baby carrots.

Cloches will help to warm the soil and bring on vegetables in time for the annual dearth.

There are some crops that will naturally fill the gap for you with little work, and this is where it gets pretty exciting: perennial plants. The best illustration of these is the humble nettle: a wonderful bringer-inner of predators of pests, like ladybirds, and the ingredient of a terrific liquid fertiliser, the nettle is also a highly nutritious leafy vegetable: soups, stir-fries, etc. The worst bit is picking them – lots of tips of shoots and lots of tingly fingers for the rest of the day unless you've remembered your gloves.

There are many plants that grow in the same place year after year (and so wouldn't be included in your rotation), sending up leaves and shoots as soon as the soil warms up. The best known are asparagus and rhubarb – wonderful plants but are they slightly limited in their range of use? Don't answer that, Yorkshire folk, with your rhubarb and kipper pie, rhubarb and black pudding pudding, etc. Spring is the forager's season – all of those young shoots ready to be plucked everywhere you look. Foraged crops are, for me, a great range of wild plants I eat when I don't have anything more interesting. Most are an 'acquired taste': it is not really surprising that Plantain, for example, a wild flower with edible leaves – not to be confused with the Caribbean giant banana – hasn't become one of our staple vegetables. Let Richard Mabey in his classic 'Food For Free' convince you otherwise. The perennial vegetables you might grow could be a combination of the best of foraged crops with a sprinkling of other selected plants.

The plants below are in addition to the perennial plants given more detailed coverage on p.116. Plant them around your plot, amongst your fruit bushes, in any spaces you can find at the periphery. All are perennials unless indicated.

Good King Henry – choose young leaves and shoots and eat like spinach.

Sorrel – use sparingly since the acid, lemony flavour is oxalic acid.

Jack-by-the-hedge / Garlic Mustard (biennial) – the leaves, used in a salad, get hotter as the season progresses.

Lime tree leaves – the leaves are largest on plants that are cut down annually (coppiced or pollarded) and are used as a lettuce substitute. Avoid collecting leaves from the suckers – the shoots clustered around the base of a lime tree – unless you can be sure they haven't been visited by the cocked legs of passing dogs.

Sweet Cicely – all parts can be eaten, the aniseedy leaves from spring onwards.

Comfrey – cook the leaves. Comfrey pakora is a favourite, though I'm not sure who with.

Salsify* (biennial) and Scorzonera* – both can be grown for their long edible roots but it is the new leaves and flowers produced the following year that can be used to fill the hungry gap.

Chicory* and Dandelion* - highly nutritious salad leaves.

Ramsons / Wild Garlic, Chives, Welsh Onion, Garlic Chives – all are perennials grown for their leaves, (the small bulbs of Welsh onion can be used later in the year).

*The leaves produced by some of these plants can be bitter. Blanching – in this context meaning excluding light from the leaves which is easiest to do with an upturned flower pot – will remove the bitterness but also reduce the nutritional content.

To summarise, in case you weren't paying attention, mind the gap in April, May and June by growing overwintering crops, very quick maturing crops and perennial plants, and by employing protection like cloches.

Green Manures, and why they are so important

At some point in the future, when we all have to rely on different organic matters like composts and manures for our supply of nutrients, they will be in short supply, purely because of demand. This will make them more expensive and harder to get hold of.

The answers include making as much of your own compost as possible.

However, it is likely that this still won't be enough. Hopefully, we will by then have overcome our squeamishness and any accompanying technical difficulties and use sewage in some form. Although this will provide plentiful nutrients it won't be a replacement for the benefits received from bulky organic matter. In the future, whatever we use, it will, in all likelihood, have to be used in conjunction with green manures. On p.181 they are discussed as part of an organic growing system. The particular properties that will make them so important include the provision of lots of plant material as organic matter to improve soil structure. This is achieved by regularly cutting down the green manure, which effectively stops it from flowering, and leaving everything where it falls, plus eventually killing and leaving the plants on the soil when you next need that land. On a small scale, the cutting is best done with shears and the killing-off with a sharp hoe or azada. If you are still a digger, then that is another method of finishing off the green manure.

Why Green Manures are the Bee's Knees:

- The leaves of growing plants will protect the soil structure that you are improving.
- They will support a vast range of organisms and reduce the loss of nutrients from a soil; rain can pass through bare soil and take nutrients with it (known as leaching) whilst roots hold on to them.
  Nitrogen is one of the more important nutrients required by plants, since it is not held well by any soils, and is easily lost: a figure of 80% lost over one winter from a bare soil is common. Plants also need it in large quantities.
- They can actually add good levels of nitrogen to the soil via nitrogen fixation. This is where the bacterium *Rhizobium* enters the roots of legumes and multiplies. The plants welcome this and grow nodules around them. The bacteria then take nitrogen from the air and fix it in their bodies, also supplying some to the plant in return for its hospitality. When we kill off the green manure this nitrogen becomes available to the crops that follow.
  The longer a nitrogen-fixing plant is growing, the better it gets at nitrogen-fixing; so, tares are great over winter and will add a little nitrogen (see table) especially in the following spring. However, red clover sown in the autumn, and left for 18 months, will add a very useful amount of nitrogen, not to mention the loads of organic matter provided during that time: potentially the equivalent of 25kg of farmyard manure per square metre. Using red clover in this way takes up a block of the rotation.

On the next page is a table of some common green manures. Most are broadcast, in that the seeds are sprinkled over the surface and gently worked in using a rake, by 'bouncing' it rather than drawing it backwards and forwards. The larger seeds need to be buried deeper than broadcasting can achieve, so have to be sown in rows (drills) close together. The sowing quantities, which are a rough guide, are in grammes per square metre.

Name	Time of sowing	Duration	Does it fix Nitrogen?	How to sow B =Broadcast R = Rows
Alfalfa	April-July	Over a year	Yes	B 2g/m^2
Buckwheat	April-Aug	1-3 months or overwinter	No	B 3g/ m^2
Clover, crimson	March-Aug	2-3 months. May overwinter	Yes	B 3g/ m^2
Clover, red	April-Aug	3-18 months	Yes	B 3g/ m^2
Field beans	Sept-Nov	Overwinter	Yes	B 5g/ m^2
Mustard	March-Sept.	1-2 months	No	B 5g/ m^2
Phacelia	March-Sept.	1-3 months. May overwinter	No	B 2g/ m^2
Tares/Vetch	March-Sept.	1-3 months. May overwinter	Yes	R 15cm apart averaging 16g/m^2

There are a few other green manures: poached egg plant (*Limnanthes*) with lovely flowers that bees and hoverflies love; Hungarian or grazing rye with a dense nutrient-trapping root system that is great for overwintering, though harder to kill off; corn salad which protects the soil over winter and is great to eat though it only produces a little organic matter for the soil. I have had great success with lentils as a green manure – using speckled Puy lentils (only the best, you know), there was great coverage, pretty speedy, too, so I'll continue to use those as a 'summer filler'. They need to be drill sown rather than broadcast.

In a no-dig system, there has to be a compromise by way of the procedures we employ. We can choose easy-to-kill annual, green manures, some of which may be killed in cold weather, but still protect the soil as a mat of dead leaves and stems. Alternatively, we can use tougher plants like red clover, that require a small amount of soil-surface disturbance in order to hoe or chop them.

Green manures aren't the whole answer: they can't produce a full range of nutrients for the crops that follow, though they can reduce their loss and, in some cases, like alfalfa, bring up nutrients from below the crop's rooting zone. They can harbour slugs (especially poached egg plant) and they may take some effort to kill off, as will the regular cutting.

When some green manure plants, like tares or rye, are dying, they can release substances that inhibit germination. This is an issue if you are sowing a crop fairly soon afterwards. Wait a month or use transplants.

However, the positives far outweigh the negatives, and there will come a point when there will probably be no choice anyway.

There is a lot of money being spent on trying to genetically engineer crop plants so that they are able to fix nitrogen directly. I wish they'd spend the time, effort and expense on developing better organic growing systems including green manures, but this brings neither the kudos nor the potentially huge financial returns of genetically-manipulated crops.

Mycorrhizal Fungi and Controlled Mess

Back in the mists of time (approximately 2012 when I started writing the first edition of this mighty tome), mycorrhizal fungi were barely mentioned let alone their range, diversity and importance. For the late-comers amongst us, mycorrhizal fungi are species of fungi which have adapted to joining forces with plants. They plug into the root systems and bring in water and nutrients from a wider area than the roots themselves have colonised. In return they receive sugars from the plants.

It is pretty obvious, even to me, that plants which are enjoying this association are going to do better: grow more strongly, cope with adverse conditions and, on the vegetable plot, crop better. This can all be done with fewer inputs from us (as happens in the wild). On top of that, the fungi can protect plant roots from pests and diseases: they're not stupid – they have a vested interest here.

Incidentally, there are apparently 25,000 km of fungal hyphae (the microscopic strands of fungi) per cubic metre of healthy soil. Those kinds of figures leave my brain hurting. Not only can't you see that huge amount, but I don't understand how it all fits in. On top of that, fungi are only one part of the whole soil food web which includes

FORGET THE VEG. - EAT THE FUNGI

worms, slugs, insects, springtails (possibly the world's most numerous multicellular organism), creatures we haven't even heard the name of let alone seen, microscopic things such as bacteria in their billions, algae, protozoa and the cutest of them all, tardigrades. Tardigrades, known as moss piglets or water bears, are virtually indestructible – they have been sent into space, deep frozen in liquid nitrogen and watched three hours of daytime television, and still survived.

All of these fit into less than 1% of the soil by volume. Now I've got a migraine coming on.

It is the balance of all of these things that make a soil healthy and all of them need looking after. It is not just plants which do so much better with a great soil food web. Witness that blackbird tugging on an elastic worm or the robin tootling away on your fork handle before diving in to grab the pupae you've just revealed.

It is why many conventional farmers 'have to' spray and feed once they have killed – or not supported – the soil food web (which they have done so by ploughing the soil and, yes, spraying and chemically fertilising). Well, as an organic gardener, you are well underway to looking after it all.

At this point, it may be worth introducing an approach to gardening called 'controlled mess'. This may help even more. One might describe the aforementioned conventional growing as 'uncontrolled mess', not in appearance which is one of lifeless monoculture including pastureland – it is the system that is a mess.

Where controlled mess and organic growing coincide is with the use of green manures, companion plants and organic matter. Where it differs is the use of

I KNOW THERE'S A CARROT IN HERE SOMEWHERE

self-seeding, weeds, no-digging, mixed cropping and a fairly slack attitude. Having plants which cover the ground and interact with soil organisms is the gold standard when it comes to mycorrhizal fungi and the soil food web. Organic matter as a mulch appears to maintain it all, too. The trickiest bit is what to do with the land when crops have finished. Definitely not digging, but a green manure or some organic matter? Either is fine if you have the time and the material, respectively. Controlled mess asks, 'What is left behind when a crop has ended?'. Some debris can simply be left indefinitely: it has been shown that dead stalks 'wick' rain down into the soil, meaning less water is left standing on the surface. Standing water doesn't stay standing for very long – it moves sideways, ultimately causing erosion.

The tops may not be dead – peas and beans are good examples. You could simply leave them there as 'occupying' plants after picking has finished or the tops can be removed for composting. The root systems left behind will decay and feed the soil. It gives the organisms associated with those plants – in this case nitrogen-fixing bacteria and mycorrhizal fungi – a chance to complete lifecycles, go dormant or be perpetuated. This also leaves the soil undisturbed and natural fissures will form as the roots decay.

Another example might be kale which, when you have given up picking tiny leaves and it has won the battle to flower in spring, can be left for bees and their mates to enjoy those flowers. The kale plants continue to occupy the land. Interestingly, members of the cabbage and beetroot families (kale is in the former) don't have mycorrhizal associations but that doesn't mean that leaving behind roots will do any harm at all. Apart from beetroot, that is, which you might want to eat at some point.

There is more to ponder. We can look at the extent of the weed cover - if it is substantial, perhaps leave it. This is heretical. But if you let the weeds grow and cover the soil, they will improve it in the same ways that green manures do and that would be wonderful: you don't even have to prepare a bed, get the seed, sow it and then wait for it to appear – the plants are already there. There are, of course, caveats. Weeds are fine as long as they are 1) not spreading or becoming too established, effectively, most perennial weeds or 2) they are not setting seed. And to enable this approach to succeed you need to be pretty hot on your weed identification.

Perennial weeds need to be removed or killed off as in 'What to do first with a new plot'. Using a fork to remove them, in a no-dig system, isn't necessarily a total disaster since it can be done carefully without turning everything upside down. Some of those kilometres of fungal hyphae will be broken and killed, though.

Annual and biennial weeds can be hoed off if they have the temerity to even think about flowering and setting seed. I remember being told that weeds in flower will continue to produce seed even after having their heads cut off. Well, more recent research says the opposite: they may be able to squeeze out a few seeds but effectively they are stopped in their tracks.

Another wonderful part of messy gardening is leaving crops and flowers to drop seeds. The salad Lamb's Lettuce (or Corn Salad) is a great example. Let some plants go to seed. Those seeds will sit there for ages before deciding to do anything. Eventually they can cover the soil later in the year or pop up amongst winter crops. Either way they are filling in gaps, can be removed at any time or can be cropped (see p.41). Flowers such as Calendula, Love-in-the-Mist or Nasturtium will shed lots of seeds after flowering – sometimes too much – but again they will fill gaps and you won't have to re-sow.

Look on Controlled Mess as horticultural improvisation: sometimes it will do the trick, other times it will look a, well, mess. Whatever happens, it is quite exciting and as a bonus you get to perpetuate that soil food web.

Growing Sustainably, introducing Veganic Growing

To put it simply, reduce what you bring onto your plot. Obviously, you may need some structural materials to make a compost bay, for example. Even then there is scope for using recycled wood (dead pallets, maybe). More useful external inputs could include other waste material such as urine, cardboard, leaves and kitchen scraps.

However, the most sustainable plot has to be where everything is re-used within the growing space. In terms of inputs to your crops, this means making them on site – fertilisers from comfrey, a wormery and nettles, and for organic matter there is home-made compost and green manures. Even seeds can be on this list, saving them from your plants one year, to use the next. See 'Seed Saving'. Home-made potting and sowing composts can be made as indicated elsewhere but if you don't have the ingredients then buying peat-free organic compost is the next best. It comes in a plastic bag. Plastic bags can be useful. It is the quantity and longevity that is the problem. Re-using them includes carrying and storage possibilities. When holes start appearing, they can be cut open and used as a cover for the compost heap, a small-area weed suppressant or a slug home (to check and clear regularly). Just be aware that as soon as they start to fragment (the plastic degrades in sunlight) get them off site. Nowadays it is possible to get bulk deliveries of compost – club together with a neighbour or three and decant it into.....old compost bags.

Don't forget to re-use spent potting compost. Where seedlings haven't deigned to show their heads and as long as no foul play is suspected (pests or diseases) then, at best it can be re-used to sow more seedlings, at worst it can be emptied out on the plot or used to line seed drills. It won't benefit a compost heap hugely since it is already composted.

Horticulture has been one of the great users of plastic. From plant pots to tools, to netting, to bags. A big problem for the organic market garden is when the public *sees* the plastic – unfortunately, leafy vegetables last umpteen times longer in a plastic bag. Any bags you somehow receive, clean them out and re-use them – you can store fresh produce better in the fridge. The same goes for containers used to propagate and grow-on plants.

Maybe the answer is to use alternatives wherever possible (think of the toilet rolls for sowing beans) and where the alternatives are inadequate or not available, go for sturdy, long-lasting, re-usable, hopefully recycled plastic which can, in the end, itself be recycled. A good example would be propagation modules. So many are sold as, effectively, one use only, it is a little distressing:

they are thin, fragile black plastic – not recyclable. On the market, obviously more expensive, are sturdy, rigid, reusable orange or green plastic module trays. Also, in the long run, they work out cheaper because they last so long.

For an organic grower, covering crops is essential to keep certain pests off. Horticultural fleece is well established to do this. But it is fragile and often lasts just one season, breaking into smaller and smaller fragments the longer you try to use it. A very fine, yes, plastic mesh – U.V. stabilised – will do the same thing but will last for many years. Look out for brands such as 'Enviromesh'.

When we talk about carbon capture and climate change, we tend to think of it as a national / international issue (if we think about it at all). Soil has the potential to be a massive store of carbon – we just need to put it there and leave it. By following a no-dig system, we would all contribute to that carbon storage. Many organic growers on a commercial scale control weeds by making repeated passes on the tractor – ploughing, harrowing, steerage hoeing. Each time this is done, fossil fuels are burnt *and* lots of air is put into the soil, both releasing carbon dioxide. It is not easy to do no-dig / no-till on a large scale without herbicides but there is much effort being put into finding a way. Conventional / chemical agriculture does no better, of course, even if it is no-till: some organic matter is added to the soil via crop residues and herbicided weeds, but the soil flora and fauna are horribly compromised by the chemical use. As gardeners, the best we can do is put organic matter on the surface of the soil from where it will be slowly processed and taken down. The amounts we use should be high, if we can get hold of it, without exceeding recommended levels that could lead to pollution.

It is worth having a look at biochar. This is semi-burnt wood which, if the energy given off to produce it is used, is pretty sustainable. It looks like the kind of charcoal you might choose to draw with. Anyway, biochar is added to the soil where it remains for many years, not only acting as a store of carbon but providing a refuge for beneficial organisms and plant nutrients in the same way that clay and humus will hold on to nutrients against leaching. This means that biochar would help enormously if the soil was very sandy or 'light' or if it has been badly treated, both physically and chemically. But adding it to any soil would be a valuable way of locking up that carbon. The price is still relatively high, especially if you want to treat a large area.

A vegan diet has been shown to be not only the healthiest but the most sustainable. Animal production and animal emissions, especially at the execrable 'factory' farms, are responsible for a significant contribution to climate change. The ethical aspect of veganism is also very interesting, when it is still mainstream to exploit and euthanise animals for, effectively, pleasure (since animal products aren't essential). If you have a conscience about climate change and the horrors  inflicted on farm animals, then it should perhaps extend to other areas of life such as growing vegetables. Would buying in manure or a fertiliser such as blood, fish and bone for your plot be supporting these systems?

But then, as growers, we are killing things all the time: weeds, soil organisms when we dig, plants we eat. A question for an individual to answer is perhaps where to draw the line. 'Which organisms *truly* suffer as a result of my vegetable growing, as opposed to "simply" dying?'

Exploiting and killing 'higher' animals is one thing, but maybe killing any non-sentient creatures is also unwise if only because they support the whole natural growing system – the food web. But then…..slugs? They are part of that web, just that some times there are so many of them.

Let's leave that one dangling in front of you like an inappropriate worm on a fishhook.

I'll shut up now – apart from this...

Last Words

What a great opportunity this has been for me to spout my opinions. Along the way I hope you weren't too offended or bored, and maybe even enjoyed the journey.

Grow your vegetables with joy. Don't be too upset when things don't go well. It will always be better next time.

Index

Page numbers in **bold** show a main reference.